Standing In The Corner

Watching Newcastle United in the Wilderness Years

By Pete McParlin

The Parrs Wood Press
Manchester

First Published 2005

THE PARRS WOOD PRESS
St Wilfrid's Enterprise Centre
Royce Road, Manchester, M15 5BJ
www.parrswoodpress.com

© Pete McParlin 2005

ISBN: 1 903158 70 2

Printed by Compass Press Ltd of London

CONTENTS

Acknowledgements

Thanks to my wife Cath for her support and understanding during the months of 'single-minded' writing that resulted in this book. And to my old mate Oges for saving me from St. James' Park exile on not one but two occasions. Without him, this story could never have been told. Respect to everyone who kept the faith throughout the lean years, in particular those whose presence made my own journey through them more fun. In football terms, 'the good old days' really were the best.

Many thanks to the Newcastle Chronicle & Journal Limited, who supplied the photographs, and I would also like to express my sincere gratitude to The Parrs Wood Press, whose help and sound advice were invaluable to me.

Introduction

The history of Newcastle United is littered with examples of the ones that got away - players sold on by the club who went on to achieve greater things elsewhere. The most famous examples are Waddle, Beardsley and Gascoigne, of course, but there have been many others. One of the least lamented escapees was Frank Clark, Newcastle United vice-captain and left back, who was given a free transfer at the end of 1974-75. Clark, who'd been an integral part of the Magpies' European Fairs Cup-winning side in 1969, was deemed to be past his best and dismissed from the club's service on the same day as Joe Harvey, manager of that same trophy-winning team. No one really noticed he'd gone. Three years later though, as Newcastle were being relegated to Division Two, Clark was winning the League title with Brian Clough's Nottingham Forest. A year after that, as United languished in mid-table mediocrity, Forest won the European Cup, and with Clark operating in his trusty left back position. Here was a player supposedly over the hill four years earlier!

Supporting a club whose judgement is as doomed as this is never going to be easy. As a season ticket holder behind me in the Gallowgate stand once remarked: "We were born to suffer". This was after a woeful performance, the first of many at the start of 1999-2000 when we'd lost 1-0 to Aston Villa and Uriah Rennie had sent off Alan Shearer. Only three months earlier, Newcastle had made their second no-show inside a year in the FA Cup Final. Losing 0-2 on the big stage twice in succession was yet another kick in the teeth for the Toon Army, who had waited since that 1969 Fairs Cup win for silverware. Only three years before, in 1996, United had blown a twelve-point lead in the Premier League title race, only to lose the championship to Manchester United on the last day of the season. We were used to that sickening phrase, "So near and yet so far!"

But suffering has to be taken in context, at least in a footballing sense. How does losing a Cup Final compare with relegation? How badly does losing a title race measure up to defeat in the play-offs at the hands of your bitterest rivals? What we count as failure as supporters of the modern Newcastle United is the disappointment of missing out on trophies. From the late seventies to early nineties, however, failure was monumental under-achievement. A football club whose stature was the equal of just about anyone in English football in 1974 was allowed to decay into mediocrity by a board of directors without the vaguest pretence of investment or ambition. And the reason for the decline of Newcastle United was different from any of the other football clubs categorised as 'sleeping giants'. Most teams, whose stature had diminished during football's decline in the seventies and eighties, had suffered from the challenge of larger rivals competing for support on their doorstep. In the North West, clubs like Preston, Blackpool and Burnley suffered at the hands of Manchester United, Liverpool and Everton. In the Midlands the culprits were Aston Villa, and in Yorkshire, Leeds. Newcastle could point to no similar example as the reason for their decline. Moreover, unlike the Prestons and Blackpools of this world, gates at St. James' Park had never dwindled close to the point of extinction. But the club continued to be run on a shoestring, with little or no money spent on new players whilst big money transfers went the other way - Newcastle United was a selling club. For ten out of the eighteen years between 1974 and 1992, we languished in Division Two and once relegation was

Introduction

first experienced in 1978, we never went close to winning any trophies! These really were the hard times for Newcastle United. The disappointments of this era outstrip anything that has occurred since, twelve-point lead or otherwise.

In his book, *Kicking With Both Feet*, Frank Clark groups football fans into six main categories based on the behaviour we are likely to display at matches. His observations are obviously made from the side of the fence occupied by the 'former pro', but nonetheless his analysis hits the mark with every faction. I like to think that I belong to his Tribesmen group, a class of fan he describes as "more supportive than all the other categories put together". According to Frank, we long for the days of the terraces. How true. This work is my recollection of the days when terraces were the main part of each and every football ground in England, when stands were the big cantilever structures down each side of the pitch and when football supporters were real fans. It is the story of the best years of my twenty-odd as a regular supporter of Newcastle United, times when the football team was, at best, a pale shadow of the supposedly poor sides of Dalglish and Gullit. Frank Clark says that the Tribesmen are under threat from rising ticket prices. This is the tale of the days it only cost a couple of quid to stand on the Gallowgate End and when you only needed a ticket for the most popular matches, like derbies with Sunderland. More than anything it is a study of what being a Newcastle supporter was all about when the football was dire but the real fans still kept going. At St. James' Park it was always an honour to stand in the corner, never a disgrace.

One

Wembley Way

Smith delivered a diagonal ball to the edge of the penalty area. Hall let it run to Keegan. A shot flashed towards the Newcastle United goal. The Magpies' goalkeeper Iam McFaul was helpless; he could only get one hand to the blistering effort, parrying it upwards into the top corner of the net.

"1-0!" declared commentator David Coleman jubilantly, continuing, "Goals came and went, and Kevin Keegan does his share." Even at the age of eight I realised that this was hardly the free verse of the poet laureate.

The goal was no more than Liverpool deserved, despite the less than impartial commentary. For all of an hour they'd run rings round their black and white opponents with no reward. Now the writing was on the wall for Newcastle, who hadn't even managed a shot on target.

"That's it!" sighed my Dad with an air of resignation. "There's no way back now. Newcastle just haven't got Supermac into the game." He was right. The Magpies' goalscoring hero in the number 9 shirt may well have scored in every round of the FA Cup up to this, the Final, but today he'd hardly had a touch. Liverpool hadn't even needed to mark him out of the game, the whole Newcastle team had frozen on the big day and the Reds, well practised in the art of peaking at the right time, had only needed to turn up. Their victory was proving a mere formality.

Wembley Way

The difference between the two teams wasn't just the quality of the players or their ability to hit peak form on the day of a Cup Final, either. The whole way the two football clubs were run was diametrically opposed. Liverpool was a forward thinking club with huge ambition, whereas Newcastle was still run in the same slapdash way it had been since the thirties. On May 4th 1974, the Magpies and the Reds still had exactly the same history of club honours - ten major domestic trophies and one UEFA/Fairs Cup each. After that day, the fortunes of both big city giants would diverge monumentally.

Of course, Newcastle hadn't won any domestic honours for nearly two decades. And now their chances of putting the skills of the FA engraver to the test were about to get even more remote.

"Heighway, could this be two? Yes!" Coleman was finding it almost impossible to disguise his joy as Liverpool's Irish winger sliced through the ineffective Newcastle defence to double their lead. Tears began to well up in the eyes of a disappointed eight-year-old. Dad just shook his head and aimed an imaginary teacup at the telly.

Outside our house in the County Durham new town of Peterlee, the vultures that had been circling since that Keegan goal half an hour earlier were now beginning their descent. This was certainly not Newcastle United territory, ten miles south of Sunderland, slap bang in the middle of the East Durham coalfield community. Here the vast bulk of the populous supported Sunderland and took great delight in watching Newcastle United, now very much the senior football club in the North East of England, being completely humiliated.

And humiliation was the word! To rub salt into the Magpies' already gaping wounds, Keegan added a third for triumphant Liverpool as the Newcastle players stood waiting for the final whistle to end their torment.

"Newcastle are undressed!" declared Coleman, himself no doubt removing his red scarf to present to old pal Emlyn Hughes as he walked up the Wembley steps to collect the cup.

The Mackems outside took great delight in signalling through our window the numbers three and nothing, indicated by the number of digits outstretched on each hand. Some also specified the numbers one and nothing, referring to Sunderland's victory over Leeds by that scoreline in the FA Cup Final of twelve months before. That had been a game in which the red and whites crossed the halfway line only twice - once to score and the other to change ends at half-time. Newcastle had attempted the same thing in 1974 and ended up getting murdered.

Only a few months later, my family was on the move - away from the Mackem hellhole that was Peterlee and up the A19 to Morpeth in South East Northumberland. Our new home was a much better place. Not just because Morpeth was a pleasant market town, a welcome change from the cardboard metropolis we'd just left, but also because it was largely devoid of that most obnoxious of species - Mackems! For me it wasn't just a step up to a more prosperous existence - a nice suburban semi with gardens front and back. It was an escape from hell and, above all, a much more agreeable environment in which to be a Newcastle supporter, only fourteen miles from St. James' Park.

My new-found obsession had lost none of its appeal following the harrowing events of early May. The added spectacle of the 1974 World Cup Finals, with the total football of Cruyff's Holland and the ruthless efficiency of West Germany, had seen to that! My own naïve hope was that Supermac could inspire Newcastle United to emulate the impressive performances of those

Wembley Way

European giants, after all he was the greatest footballer in the world. Better than Cruyff, Beckenbauer, or any of them. How much I had still to learn! There was one overriding reason why this never could be... inconsistency, the one thing the Germans and Dutch didn't practice, was the Magpies' hallmark and the season to come would see it demonstrated to a previously unprecedented degree!

1974-75 saw Newcastle flatter to deceive in every sense of the word. In both cup competitions, United did the hard part first, beating strong opposition in the early rounds only to fall to minnows later on. The League Cup saw the Magpies dispose of Nottingham Forest, QPR and Fulham, all by convincing scorelines, only to fall to humble Chester City in the quarter-finals. Had United progressed, they'd have been the only First Division team left in the semis! The FA Cup wasn't much less disappointing. After the 2-0 defeat of Manchester City at Maine Road in round three, Newcastle fell to Third Division Walsall at the next hurdle. I would soon learn that pride so often came before a fall for the black and whites!

League form was even more bewildering, as Newcastle stumbled through the season well clear of danger but without ever managing to get into the top half of the Division One table. United had developed a habit that niggled away at the St. James' Park faithful enough for them to call for, and eventually get, the head of veteran manager Joe Harvey. That trait was their ability to beat top teams one week and then lose to more modest opposition the next. Never the kind of form likely to mount a title challenge! But to a nine-year-old fanatic, seeing your team beating the best sides in the land was every bit as good as winning major trophies. During 74-75, Newcastle successively knocked Ipswich, Manchester City and Liverpool off top spot in the division, the latter by 4-1. In addition, the Magpies retained the largely meaningless Texaco Cup and the colossal figure of Supermac stood proud as the leading scorer in Division One. All of these were feats that warranted fevered celebrations in my inexperienced eyes!

Of course, playing the game with my new friends on the streets and playing fields of Morpeth was of equal importance to following proper football. Like all boys of that age my only ambition was to become a professional footballer, not just any sort of player, but centre forward for Newcastle - the next Supermac! Needless to say, I understood that this burning ambition would require one virtue in excess of any other - practice. And so, at all times outside of the classroom, I felt bound to meet this obligation - in the school yard, on playing fields and under street-lit patches of grass after dark - playing out my dreams in the guise of my black and white heroes, Malcolm Macdonald et al!

The weekend was the best time for playing football, of course, and Saturdays in particular were regimented to allow the beautiful game in all its forms to fill every minute of the day. Every week at 10am sharp, my pals Burkey and Vince would call and off we'd troop for a kick around on the local playing field. This was a magnificent place, appropriately nicknamed "Wembley" by the local children. It gave us acres of room for playing on and had a single goal sited near the middle of the grass. The main advantage in this was that there was no pitch, discouraging older children and youths, and leaving the whole place free for us to enjoy, hassle free. Those weekly two-hour 'training' sessions seemed to last for ever as we played out a variety of scenarios - tackling, headers and volleys, shooting - with all of us equally happy to take the part of Supermac guiding a header towards goal or McFaul diving to the left or right to keep it out.

Wembley Way

The next vital event of Saturday was *Football Focus*, for which we always ended our Wembley session by 12 noon prompt. The format for the programme was not dissimilar from today, consisting of international action, interviews and replays from *Sportsnight* and *Match of the Day*. After lunch, we could either restart our 'training' on one of the nearby grass verges or settle down to watch for scores coming in whilst *Grandstand* splurged out its live fare of Rugby League and Racing. This was the most important ninety minutes of the week and the tension we endured between 3pm and 4.30 was far greater than during the weekly retreat behind the settee for *Dr. Who*! The adrenaline rushed and our nerves jangled every time that little black box appeared at the bottom of the screen with the ominous message of "Football Latest".

If that was bad, then *Final Score* was worse. A camera watched an old fashioned teleprinter, hawk-like, as it tapped out results coming in from across the land. The wait for Newcastle's score often felt like an eternity as the cursor rattled back and forth, like the sights on the gun in *The Golden Shot*, and in 74-75 it truly was a lottery as to their eventual fate! Finally, as daylight faded, the weekly campaign would begin to persuade my parents to let me stay up for the magic that was *Match of the Day*. My efforts were more likely to be realised if Dad, a merchant seaman, was at home. But when he wasn't, at least a Newcastle game would guarantee success. Unfortunately their indifferent form meant the Magpies made only two appearances that season and my late nights were kept to a minimum!

Sundays offered a better chance for me to see my idols in action on the telly. Tyne Tees Television's programme *Shoot*, which went out at 2pm, always featured extended highlights of a Newcastle, Sunderland or Middlesbrough home game. As St.

Standing in the Corner

James' Park was only a mile from Tyne Tees' studios on City Road, it was usually the black and whites that were featured, much to the wholly unjustified complaints of residents on the banks of the Wear and Tees! It was just as well as there was never any chance I would get to see Newcastle United in the flesh in those days. Dad's job meant he was rarely around long enough to cope with such things as taking his eldest son to football in the dark days of terrace hooliganism. Added to that, my dyed-in-the-wool Magpie uncles on my mam's side, all four of them, had long since emigrated to such far flung places as Suffolk, Blackpool, Rochdale and West Yorkshire and all had kids of their own to consider. So it would just have to be worship from afar. But as the summer of 1975 spawned a new season, a new manager had arrived at Newcastle, for whom any thought of idolatry was a complete abhorrence.

Gordon Lee was a largely unheard of coach, who'd just steered an ailing Blackburn Rovers back out of the wastelands of Division Three. Supermac's first reaction was to ask, "Gordon Who?" when told the identity of the new United supremo! Hardly a glowing compliment, but what else could be expected when a superstar player found out his new boss was an unknown. Unfortunately, Malcolm Macdonald would soon know exactly who Gordon Lee was as, hardly having got off great start, their relationship deteriorated still further throughout 1975-76. The manager's public sniping at his ostentatious striker was never likely to hide the truth and it soon became common knowledge that the two men were far from bosom buddies!

Lee's belief that stars were only found in the sky, fostered in the workmanlike environment of the Third Division, didn't fit easily with Macdonald's big star, big mouth image. The two were immediately at odds as Lee cleared out what remained of Joe Harvey's early seventies outfit. Supermac had enjoyed a productive four-year spell with strike partner "Hallelujah!" John Tudor and provider Terry Hibbitt, but at the start of 75-76 Lee sold both men whilst still in their prime. Tudor's replacement was university graduate and journeyman pro Alan Gowling, a gangling figure who quickly assumed a role as the voice of the Magpies' playing staff. Along with other new players signed in the death throes of the Harvey regime, Gowling formed an 'inner circle', much to Gordon Lee's appreciation, and Malcolm Macdonald suddenly found himself an outsider at his beloved St. James' Park.

In typical fashion, Supermac did his talking with his feet as well as his big gob, netting a staggering five times for England in a Nations Cup Qualifier against Cyprus. He also hit the net repeatedly for Newcastle, as did Gowling, and though the Magpies failed to improve on the previous season's league form, they did at least make significant progress in both cup competitions. United reached the final of the League Cup and the FA Cup sixth round in 75-76 before, on successive weekends, a flu-ravaged squad went down to Manchester City and Derby respectively. The cup runs may well have saved Gordon Lee's bacon, as his brief had been to turn round the club's fortunes in the league. But opinions in the boardroom would be the least of the new manager's problems, for what he was about to do next would condemn him to eternal damnation in the eyes of the St. James' Park faithful.

By now, my own football had taken a turn for the better. The Saturday mornings at 'Wembley' had given way to more serious training sessions organised by the father of one of the lads at our school, St. Robert's primary in Morpeth. The benefit to the under-11 team was momentous, as it went the whole season undefeated with Burkey, the team captain and top

Standing in the Corner

scorer, and Vince and myself, both a year younger, making two appearances each. It was, however, to be an unrealistic prelude to the real world of competitive school football. Matches were only usually organised against other Catholic schools in the area, and when we did encounter a 'proper team', hammering Chantry Middle School 13-2, they turned out to be one of the worst teams in the county! We would all get a rude awakening before 1976 was out. But all that mattered for now was that our 'playing careers' were underway. Professional football beckoned, for sure, and street corner kickabouts had been consigned to history.

The summer of that year saw Burkey, Vince and myself preparing for the ordeal of moving to a much larger school, the newly opened St. Benedict's Middle in nearby Ashington. But if this prospect was traumatic, it was nothing compared to the bombshell about to be dropped at St. James' Park during arid months of the close season. The feud that had been simmering between Supermac and Gordon Lee had suddenly boiled over and the upshot was that Newcastle United's 1970s superhero was abruptly sold to Arsenal for £333,333. Without a shadow of a doubt, this was treason of the worst kind. The fans were in hysteria and bookmakers slashed the odds on Newcastle to be relegated to 4-1. Lee had got his way, but how would his starless Newcastle United fare without their goalscoring talisman? Surprisingly, the answer was very well! The Magpies enjoyed their best league season in over twenty years as Gordon Lee's black and white army mounted a stirring title challenge in the opening two thirds of 1976-77. It was, however, only to be a very brief period of success. The consequences of Lee's actions in the transfer market, both outward and inward, would have a profound effect on the fortunes of Newcastle United F.C. Worst of all, the man himself would long since have departed the scene when the proverbial eventually hit the fan. Lee may well have ridden out the storm in 1976, but in '77 he really would set the cat among the pigeons!

Whilst Newcastle United were enjoying a secure existence in the upper reaches of Division One, for Vince and myself, life was far less comfortable playing for St. Benedict's under 11s in the East Northumberland Secondary Schools' League. Our first two fixtures saw the eventual winners and runners-up visit our Ashington playing field and administer a stiff dose of reality. Newbiggin Middle and Newminster, a school from Morpeth, handed us hammerings to the tune of 6-0 and 5-0 respectively. That season with St. Roberts had prepared us for nothing like this! At least our third game - Chantry at home - offered some hope, but could their current under 11s be as bad as the class of 75-76? Fortunately, they were and St. Benedict's archaic WM formation at last found success in the form of a welcome 2-0 victory. After that, the defeats resumed and by the end of January we were rooted to the foot of the eight-team table with only two points to show for our efforts.

By contrast Newcastle United were having an excellent season, tucked in behind pacesetters Liverpool and Manchester City, and very much in title contention with a third of the season still to go. The Toon Army had all but forgiven Gordon Lee for selling Supermac, after all the Magpies had never been involved in a championship race during his five-year spell at the club. Maybe we would at last see some more silverware to add to the Fairs Cup of eight years before. The manager however, had other ideas. In the wake of a rare home defeat to Man City, Lee sensationally quit, having been lured to take over from Billy Bingham at mid-table Everton. Not surprisingly, there was outrage. To this day, if he were to come back to Tyneside, Gordon Lee would have to do so in disguise. How could he get rid of Newcastle's most prized asset and then not stay on to complete the rebuilding job? Think of how we felt about Ruud Gullit and his dealings with Alan Shearer in the late nineties. Then think how much more we'd have hated him if he'd actually sold Newcastle's most influential player! Lee's actions confirmed the fans' worst suspicions and ensured that a dark border of infamy will forever surround his chapter in the history of Newcastle United.

And the trouble wasn't finished there either. The footballers Lee had actively encouraged to initiate a players' forum now mounted a conspicuous campaign aimed at getting Lee's assistant Richard Dinnis appointed as his successor. With Gowling and club captain Geoff Nulty at the centre of the conspiracy, they used a variety of tactics more suited to a British Leyland factory floor, including the threat of strike action and mass transfer requests. Against their better judgement, the Newcastle United board of directors caved in and appointed Dinnis, a schoolteacher by trade, as caretaker boss. At least he had the intelligence not to upset the balance of the team during the run-in. For, whilst Liverpool were now far too strong to be overhauled as champions, the Magpies managed to hang on desperately for fifth spot in the division and gain a lucrative place in the following season's UEFA Cup.

Meanwhile, another schoolteacher was improving the fortunes of St. Benedict's under-11s. Mr. McNeill scrapped our ineffective WM formation in favour of a modern 4-3-3 and the turnaround was immediate. The first result was still a defeat, but a highly respectable one, going down only 1-3 at title-chasing Newminster. After that, the results just kept coming. 1-0 against Hirst Park, a 0-0 draw in the return at Chantry and then my own personal triumph, a 2-1 victory over

Alexandra Middle in which I scored the first goal and provided a pinpoint cross for the second! Finally we beat Bothal Middle 1-0 on their own turf and we'd clawed our way back up to fifth, only missing a top half finish on goal difference.

If 76-77 left a satisfying feeling, then the following campaign would be one of pure frustration. For Newcastle United the consequences of Lee's flawed policies and the fall-out from that unsightly player-power episode resulted in a disastrous start to 1977-78. At the end of the preceding season, not without misgivings, the board had appointed the amiable Dinnis as full-time manager under further pressure from the playing staff. Their reluctance was soon vindicated as the Magpies proceeded to stumble out of the blocks and fall flat on their faces in the late summer of 1977. Following a 3-2 home win over Leeds, Newcastle then failed to gain a single point from their next ten games and soon found themselves embroiled in a tormenting relegation battle. After being knocked out of the UEFA Cup 5-2 on aggregate by French side Bastia, and with only five points from thirteen games in the league, Newcastle sacked Dinnis. His appointment had been a disaster, as had the performances of the players that had so actively campaigned for it.

Having been managed in the preceding few months, first by Mr. Silly and then by Mr. Nice, Newcastle now looked to Mr. Nasty to put their house in order. The board wanted no repeat of the player antics seen during the last managerial change and looked to a hard man to kick Gowling, Nulty and co. up the arse and get them doing exactly what they were supposed to do - playing football. Bill McGarry, who'd made his name bouncing teacups off dressing room walls at Molineux, entered St. James' Park in November 1977 with the brief not only of halting the relegation slide, but also sorting out some of the players indexed under the letter W in the Newcastle United yearbook! McGarry fulfilled the second part with ease, dispatching Gowling and Nulty to pastures new, followed by half the Lee/Dinnis first team. The first bit was going to be much harder. Replacements were not the best, and though one of them would go on to become a top class player elsewhere and then return many years later to be a star at Newcastle, the season would plumb still greater depths and end in ignominious relegation with a record low of just 22 points.

A six-year term of imprisonment in Division Two was the sentence imposed on the Magpies for the injudicious appointment of Gordon Lee and its unforeseen consequences. As a result, Newcastle lost their position as one of the nation's foremost sides and the underambition of the club's directors would become increasingly obvious in the long struggle to get back up into the top flight. Both as a supporter and at playing level, football had become a source of repeated disappointment. Failure at any level is a bitter pill to swallow, a situation compounded for me by the fact that the beautiful game was now vying for my sporting attentions with a newfound passion for angling. The forthcoming distractions of adolescence could easily have taken away my infatuation with Newcastle United forever, but ironically it would be that sense of failing that restored my love of football. I would soon learn that battling on through adversity is the key to success in any sport - or at least to the enjoyment of it. The fate of my own football career was about to see to that.

Whilst Bill McGarry's first full season in charge of United would be one merely of consolidation, at St. Benedict's the 1978-79 season dawned amid great expectation. Although our under-13s team lacked depth, by now we possessed one outstanding player and a handful who were of borderline county trials standard. If we could only get results against some of the better sides, we might just be in with an outside chance this time round. Unfortunately, this expectation proved wildly optimistic - we never got close to a result against the top teams and were muscled-out of fourth spot again by the more physical Hirst Park. The season represented a watershed for me, as my personal confrontations with some of the better players in the league led me to realise I was never going to be good enough to play professional football. That dream was over. From now on the playing side of the game would become less serious. But with Newcastle only able to finish eighth in their first season in Division Two, the supporting side would have to be tempered with a certain amount of philosophical detachment as well. The carefree days of childhood had collapsed into the harsh realities of teenage life.

As Newcastle prepared for a second season outside the top flight, my move up to St. Benet Biscop High School in 1979 was to introduce me for the first time to life outside of the first team. The competition for places in this school's under-14s team was tough and despite my middle school pedigree, I only made one appearance for St. Benet's in 1979-80. I wasn't completely missing out on competitive football though, as by now I was also playing regularly for the under-16s team of a local village, Longhorsley. This was football at its most laidback, with informal matches that fitted nicely with my new philosophy that the game should be fun. I was enjoying my football more than at any time since I was nine or ten. If only Newcastle could increase that feel-good factor with the sort of form that could deliver promotion.

Amazingly, in the opening months of 1979-80, the Magpies appeared to be doing exactly that! McGarry's

Standing in the Corner

unlikely strike pairing of former Nottingham Forest League Champion Peter Withe and ex-Ellington Colliery pit deputy, Alan Shoulder, was setting Division Two alight. Their return of nine and sixteen goals respectively had propelled the Magpies to the top of the table, and as Sunderland were put to the sword on New Year's Day 1980, a return to the top flight after only a two-year absence seemed a very realistic prospect. Unfortunately, the dream was to become a nightmare in the second half of the season. Deprived of key players through injury, United slid down the table on the run-in and could finish only ninth. Agonisingly, Sunderland snatched promotion on the last day of the season. Things couldn't get much worse than that! The lot of the Newcastle United fan was at its lowest ebb for a generation.

At the start of 1980-81, McGarry was sacked and Arthur Cox named as Newcastle's fourth new manager in five years. The man now trusted with the job of turning the Magpies round was another uncompromising character, but for the first two seasons of his reign the club's fortunes on the pitch changed little. United were now as good as broke and the new boss had to suffer the indignity of shopping in the bargain basement for players to further the cause. Ironically, the first new signing of the Cox era cost nothing, as the much-maligned scouting system discovered a gem on their doorstep that would turn out to be one of the finds of the decade. What's more, United were about to steal a march on their recently promoted rivals and insert the first piece in a jigsaw that would eventually show a much brighter future of promotion and a return to the top flight.

Bill McGarry's last act before the axe had fallen had been to run the rule over one Chris Waddle, a prolific forward in the Northern League with Tow Law, who'd twice been rejected by Sunderland. Despite having had his trial spell curtailed by a crude training ground tackle, McGarry had been sufficiently impressed by Waddle to offer him terms. After the departure of the old boss, all that was left for Cox to do was tie up the loose ends. Within weeks Waddle was in the first team and the rest would be history. For the short term at least, Sunderland's loss would very much be the Magpies' gain, as Chris Waddle became the first of a succession of superstars to grace St. James' Park in the 1980s.

As 1980-81 and 81-82 yielded further mid-table positions for the Magpies, the first team squad was at last beginning to resemble the famous line-up that would gain promotion in 1984. Apart from Waddle, names like Carney, Carr, Mills, Saunders, Trewick and Wharton all featured regularly on the team-sheet, along with that of Imre Varadi, who had become Newcastle's first effective centre forward since the departure of Peter Withe. Whilst up to now Cox had been slowly getting things right again on the pitch for United, frustration had been growing on the terraces and fans had voted with their feet. Average gates had dwindled to below 20,000 for the first time in the club's history. But if the Magpies' supremo had up to now been methodical, what he was about to do next would be so sudden and mind-blowingly unexpected as to launch the black and white army into orbit!

Two

Keegan

Up to now, my footballing experience had been entirely as a player with a keen but distant interest in the fortunes of one professional football club. I'd never been to see that football club play, home or away, but by 1982 had myself played in the region of 60 competitive matches at school and boys' club level. I'd even played competitive football whilst on a school exchange trip in France! Such a background usually leads a footballer that isn't of professional standard on to a career in local leagues without the time to dedicate to being a football supporter. So how exactly did I end up becoming a dedicated fan on the terraces, rather than playing extensively in the Saturday and Sunday afternoon leagues? There was one single event that changed my outlook on football and to this day it still ranks as one of the most important episodes in the history of Newcastle United.

By the summer of 1982, few people away from Tyneside were taking much notice of the once famous Magpies. Four long years of incarceration in the Second Division had resulted in a club that was a shadow of its former self stagnating in mid-table mediocrity. Whilst Arthur Cox was certainly making headway, it would take more than just honest graft to get United back into the promised land of Division One. What was needed was some flare, the very thing lacking at St. James' Park since Gordon Lee had disposed of the last of it back in the late 70s. Sure,

Keegan

Chris Waddle was one for the future, but he was still a raw talent and could use some experience alongside him to help fulfill his potential. The problem was that Newcastle United lacked either the profile or, more critically, the cash to attract such players to the club. Signings had even had to be abandoned at the eleventh hour because the club had been unable to raise the money to make the deal go through. The thought of Newcastle being able to sign a genuine superstar, bigger even than those they'd got rid of in the decade past, would have appeared to most people in 1982 as nothing short of a bad joke.

In Arthur Cox, however, Newcastle had a manager prepared to risk his own credibility on a gamble so outrageous and with so little chance of success as to render him a laughing stock if it didn't come off. Cox had heard that Kevin Keegan, England captain and not so long ago European Footballer of the Year, was unsettled at Southampton and keen on a move following a disappointing World Cup Finals in Spain. The manager approached the board, who were obviously interested, if more than a little sceptical about his proposal. Southampton had set Keegan's transfer fee at £100,000, which was no object, even to the cash-strapped Magpies. But suppose Keegan was interested, how could Newcastle afford his wages? Luckily, Cox had that one covered as well. With shirt sponsorship having only recently been sanctioned in the Football League, Newcastle had immediately signed a deal with brewing giant and next-door neighbour, Scottish & Newcastle Breweries. If they could become involved, then Keegan's salary might just be affordable too.

As it turned out, Keegan was interested. He obviously realised his career was nearing an end and was keen on the challenge of helping to turn round a sleeping giant like Newcastle. As expected, KK's wage demands were high but the little maestro himself came up with a proposition that would ensure the club got its man. He suggested a form of bonus payment linked directly to the percentage increase on the St. James' Park gate that his presence in the team would surely guarantee. Brilliant! It meant that everyone was a winner and, true to expectation, Newcastle's attendances did rise by nearly 100%! Keegan signed on the dotted line and an incredible new chapter in the history of Newcastle United had opened.

So the deal was all done and dusted and, after much speculation, Kevin Keegan was unveiled as Newcastle United's newest player to an astonished media at a press conference at Gosforth Park Hotel. Of course, the response from the long-suffering Toon Army was even more ecstatic. The rush for season tickets was as mad as it would be eleven years later when United were preparing to take their bow in the Premiership. Everything was now set for the spectacle of the first game of the season, at home to would-be promotion rivals QPR on August 28th.

In the short time between the sensational Keegan swoop and the opening fixture, Cox had done his best to acquire further experienced players to add to what was still a squad in dire need of strengthening. Defenders Jeff Clarke and John Craggs were added and eventually Terry McDermott would return after seven sensational years at Liverpool, joining tireless midfield ball winner David McCreery to give the midfield the resolve it would need. For now, though, all hopes were pinned on Keegan. The rest of the side, even including Waddle, were not in his class. But would the presence of greatness in their midst be a catalyst to inspire them to raise their games?

The opening game of the season promised to be a firecracker and what a match it would be for me to make my first visit to the hallowed St. James' Park.

Keegan

Although I possessed an abundance of experience playing junior football in all its forms, I was a complete novice when it came to watching real football on the terraces. Until August 1982, the telly had provided me with my only impression of professional football and, of course, the sights, the sounds, the smell of mud, just like a playing field on a damp Sunday afternoon and the whole reality of just being there, was a world apart from what I'd expected. The first shock was the sheer volume of people walking along the streets leading up to the ground. There was singing, there was shouting and of course there were the drunks staggering to and from local hostelries. I was sixteen and although alcohol was something I'd come across, laughing at a mate whose eyes were gone and whose speech was slurring after a can and a half of McEwan's Best Scotch was a world away from the intoxicated wobble of The Strawberry's piss-heads. I was used to that sickly feeling from pre-match nerves when I was playing, but here I just felt scared.

By the time I got inside, the crowd on 'the corner' section of the wide open Gallowgate End was already large, making it impossible to get much of an idea of exactly what I was standing on. It felt like giant concrete steps that radiated up the slope in an arc away from the corner flag. My companions for the big game, some mates from Morpeth, at least had a little experience of 'going to the match' and we squeezed our way through the mass of bodies, down the steps to stand in front of one of the chest-high concrete crush barriers that appeared to litter the large terrace. And our choice of location was quickly proven wise as, with three quarters of an hour still to go to kick-off, the ground, already packed, was getting fuller by the minute.

High up above us, at the top of the terracing, was where the most vociferous supporters - and many of the most drunken ones - were gathering. If I turned half way round I could just about see them, some standing aloft on top of the barriers, singing and bouncing around under the ever watchful gaze of the local constabulary. The reason we were standing in front of the barrier soon became evident as a loud "Aaaaghhh!" spluttered from behind us and was followed by a mass of bodies spilling down the terrace. What I had just witnessed, of course, was a crowd surge, caused as each supporter involved displaced the person in front of them, every one maintaining its footing courtesy of the body it had just collided with. I would eventually come to understand that in an average St. James' Park crowd of, say, 20,000, crowd surges could be fun but in a full house they were, rightly, something to avoid.

With the gate approaching 36,000 this most certainly was a full house and by now, five to three, the streets outside the ground were a hive of activity as latecomers scurried around trying to find a turnstile that would still allow them through. Thousands were left locked outside. Now there came a much louder roar than the one half an hour earlier. This time it was the real thing, not just drunken high jinx, as two rows of players filed out of the tunnel in the middle of the old grey West Stand. The two teams peeled off in opposite directions as they made their way out for the warm-up, Newcastle lining up with Hardwick, Craggs, Saunders, Trewick, Clarke, Haddock, Keegan, Martin, Varadi, Cartwright and Waddle. But it was just one man of those eleven that everyone had come to see.

"Keegan, Keegan..." roared the crowd as Tyneside's number one superhero made his way out to the centre circle for pleasantries and the flip of the coin. The stewards and police manning the touchlines were having their work cut out trying to prevent good-natured incursions onto the pitch. Numerous fans, over-eager to pay homage, were trying their damnedest to make it out into the middle to greet their new hero. But, far from confrontational, the atmosphere remained lighthearted, if boisterous, a fitting way to start-off Kevin Keegan's involvement at Newcastle United. Now the tension rose still further as the two sides lined up to kick off.

As with so many landmark games, the match itself was no classic. The two sides were evenly matched and chances were at a premium, but it took just one moment of sheer brilliance to elevate the whole spectacle to its rightful level of magnificence. The move for the only goal of the game started on fifteen minutes when John Craggs punted a ball forward from the right-back position in the direction of Keegan. KK flicked the ball on to Varadi who knocked it back into the little man's path as he spun off his marker and went in on goal. One-on-one with the QPR keeper, Keegan showed the composure of a world-class striker as he drew Hucker and slotted the ball underneath his sprawling body into the net. As the ball crossed the line, the reaction in the Gallowgate End was pure ecstasy. Fans leaped around in uncontrolled joy, crowd surges spilling down the terrace from all directions. I just retained my balance long enough to see Keegan continue his run and disappear into the crowd down in front of me. What a start, St. James' Park hadn't seen anything like it since Supermac scored a hat-trick on his debut, ironically against Keegan's Liverpool in 1971.

Impressive though the first game had been, to begin with, the good times were only temporary: one star player and a handful of journeymen pros couldn't change a mid-table side into promotion material overnight. Newcastle's form remained indifferent throughout the early part of the season until the arrival of the more influential McDermott and McCreery brought an upturn in our fortunes. In the second half, United picked up but, in spite of now looking the best side in the division, we had left it too late to manage to climb any higher than fifth. Arthur Cox now set about persuading his prize asset to commit to a further one-year contract in order for a more sustained promotion push in 1983-84. Keegan eventually agreed but not without certain preconditions. Inserted into the small print, the new deal included several escape clauses and a commitment from the club to invest more heavily in the transfer market.

Cox's first two forays were, on paper, the sort of ambitious signings Keegan had demanded. Full-backs John Ryan and Malcolm Brown arrived at a combined cost of £325,000, but neither would actually figure significantly in 1983-84. Meanwhile, Imre Varadi had been allowed to leave the club to make way for a new striker to partner King Kev. Initially, Newcastle had trailed Cambridge's lanky goalscorer George Reilly, a player who would eventually arrive at St. James' Park eighteen months late. In the meantime, he was stolen by First Division Watford, although, in hindsight, what exactly Cox was thinking about in trying to pair him with Keegan is anybody's guess! A far more suitable alternative was the eventual outcome and the Magpies' boss was about to unwittingly add a third superstar name to the Newcastle United playing staff, as his relentless search for new talent gathered pace.

Peter Beardsley, like Waddle, had grown up within a few miles of St. James' Park, and like his future England team mate, had slipped through the net of the Magpies' scouting system. But Beardsley's travels in search of a top class career had taken him far further afield than Tow Law. Having been taken out of the amateur game by ex-Magpies skipper Bob Moncur at Carlisle, Pedro had moved on to Vancouver Whitecaps in Canada. Ron Atkinson had just run the rule over

Beardsley for Manchester United and on this occasion, Big Ron's judgement was found lacking. Atkinson rejected the former Wallsend Boys' Club junior and Arthur Cox swooped immediately to bring Pedro back home.

It was the final piece in the jigsaw that had seen Cox transform Newcastle from dull mid-table under-achievers to an exciting attacking side capable of taking on anyone in Division Two. In a start not unlike that of Linford Christie, United shuddered out of the blocks in August 1984 before igniting the afterburners and screaming into the lead in late September and October. United reeled off six straight wins as the season entered its most significant phase, including a monumental 5-0 victory over promotion favourites Manchester City at St. James' Park. That game signalled the arrival, in no uncertain terms, of Peter Beardsley as he helped himself to a hat-trick in the sort of style that would quickly become his trademark. All three goals were typical Beardsley: the first saw him go past one defender, then the keeper, before drilling the ball past three City players on the line; the second typified his never-say-die attitude and the third was a clinical finish after accepting a Waddle pass to put him in on goal. The Magpies were now steaming at full speed towards promotion.

Although their momentum was interrupted, briefly, by two away defeats at the eventual Division Two champions and runners-up, Chelsea and Sheffield Wednesday, Newcastle's progress was soon back on track. By Christmas, United were in a two-horse race with Manchester City for the third promotion place, with the unfancied Grimsby Town and Carlisle hanging on to their coat tails. There was now a brief interlude as Newcastle prepared to travel to Anfield to take on Liverpool in the FA Cup third round. It was a game charged with atmosphere, not least because of

Standing in the Corner

Keegan's return to his old club and the obvious echoes of that FA Cup Final of ten years before. And just to add to the tension, the contest was being televised live on Friday night TV. In the end, the match itself was a non-event, Liverpool outclassing the Magpies 4-0, although this was no disgrace. The FA Cup was the only competition The Reds didn't win in 1984, as they swept-up a unique European Cup, League title and League Cup treble. At least Newcastle's Toon Army, camped in the Anfield Road End, won the contest between the fans. As became customary throughout the rest of the Eighties, the black and whites comprehensively out-sang their red counterparts, with the favourite on the night being, "We've got more fans than you, Liverpool, Liverpool..." to the tune of a British Airways advert!

The only blessing from the Liverpool defeat was that it meant there would be no added distraction in this most crucial of seasons and Newcastle were now able to concentrate solely on the league. For Keegan, however, the Liverpool match had been a watershed. In the eighteen months since he'd last played against top class opposition, the Magpies' main man realised that the years were finally catching up. At the age of 33, KK announced that he would be hanging up his boots for good at the end of the season. This gave the promotion push still more impetus. What more fitting way for King Kev to round-off his glittering career than by leading the Magpies back up to their rightful place in the top division?

And United took to their task with style and conviction. As they stacked-up the points total, Chris Waddle and Peter Beardsley emerged emphatically as the ultimate successors to Keegan's throne. All three Newcastle strikers were on fire, bagging a total of 65 out of the Magpies' 85 league goals between them. The highlights of the promotion run-in in the spring of

Keegan

1984 were numerous. A crucial 2-1 away win at City, 3-1 over Middlesbrough and the 5-1 demolition of Carlisle on Easter Monday. But it was the last home game of the season against Brighton that everyone will remember. Division One status had been mathematically guaranteed the previous Monday night and a promotion party involving a gate of over 36,000 had gathered to celebrate and witness the historic moment of Kevin Keegan's final competitive game.

On an afternoon choked with emotion, Keegan led out his Newcastle teammates for a lap of honour before the large crowd. They then proceeded to lay on top-level entertainment to the celebrating hordes in a manner another Magpies side would repeat in similar circumstances nine years later. The principal performers were, of course, the maestro KK himself, Waddle and Beardsley, who predictably each claimed a goal in the 3-1 triumph. What a way to finish. Apart from the glorious way it ended the Magpies' six-year absence from the top flight, the symbolism the match entailed was every statistician's dream. Keegan scoring in his last game, as well as his first; the three musketeers all finding the target again and United finishing the season a clear ten points ahead of Man City in third place.

Another lap of honour followed at the end of the match and a final farewell to Keegan was staged when Liverpool, by then Champions of both England and Europe, took part in an exhibition match at St. James' Park after the end of the season. It all ended in truly spectacular fashion as King Kev left the pitch in a helicopter, departing the Gallowgate arena for, as far as anyone present could have known, the final time. Newcastle United was a much healthier football club than the one he'd arrived at two years before. For the St. James' Park faithful, the good times were back!

Three

Sack Jack

Tyneside had been nearing fever pitch as the last matches of 83-84 were played out. When the finish line was crossed, it signalled the sort of outpouring of emotions unseen since the Fairs Cup was brought back in June 1969. The long suffering Toon Army had waited an awful long time for an excuse for a party and nothing was going to stop them now! The celebrations lasted well into the summer months and some even began getting carried away by all the festivities, raving about what great achievements lay ahead in the new season to come.

The reality of the situation was not lost on some of the more experienced heads at St. James' Park, however. The club was still run by the same group of underambitious directors that had allowed it to become bogged down in the Division Two quagmire. It had taken the guile of Cox and the magic of Keegan to stop the rot, but the board lacked that sort of pragmatism, and more importantly the finances to support it. If getting out of Division Two had been tough, then staying in the top flight would be tougher, but the directors at St. James' were set in their ways and determined to run the club in the way they saw fit. It would not go into debt to buy new players, even if that debt could immediately be recouped at the turnstiles, as had been shown with Keegan. But now Keegan was gone, surely some new blood was essential, especially as the step up to Division One

Sack Jack

status was a completely new world for most of the existing squad.

Cox had been campaigning tirelessly to be given more cash to spend, but the more he tried, the more his pleas fell on deaf ears. The board even had the cash from Keegan's sell-out 'testimonial' jangling in their pockets, gifted to the club by the great man, but still they refused to budge. Finally, the unthinkable happened. Within weeks of promotion having been clinched, Arthur Cox quit Newcastle, lured by the challenge of re-awakening yet another sleeping giant, Third Division Derby County. The fans greeted the news with disbelief. Six long years it had taken to restore top-flight football to St. James' Park, and yet within six weeks the two principal architects of the Newcastle United revival had both taken their leave of the club. But the board were not about to allow the crisis to become an emergency. They had the very man lined up for the vacant manager's job and he would play things just the way they wanted. In less than a week, the position had been filled and by their own standards, the club appeared to have moved ambitiously to fill the void.

In Jack Charlton, Newcastle United had not just attracted a big name to become the new manager; they'd lured an authentic Geordie and a self-confessed lifelong Magpies fan. On the face of it, United seemed to have come out of the whole business of Cox's resignation smelling of roses, but behind the scenes things were still far from secure as they prepared for their big return to Division One. There was still no real money available for the new boss to spend on players; Charlton later said he was only offered £200,000 - hardly enough to buy one quality player in 1984's marketplace. But what Newcastle did possess in their new man was one of the shrewdest tacticians in the game. In his first spell of coaching, down the road at Middlesbrough, Big Jack had turned round a mid-table Division Two side, making them champions in his first season and top seven in the First Division in his second. And he'd done it making only a single sortie into the transfer market. A tactical brainwave had been the key to Boro's success in which a single midfield player had been used to run through opposition defences from deep, springing the offside trap time after time. Here, it would seem, was the ideal man to make the most of Newcastle's inexperienced squad, but what sort of tactical vision would Charlton dream up?

Lacking any sort of big target man to play as an out-and-out centre forward, Jack's thinking focussed on how to best use the talented Waddle and Beardsley as attacking players. His solution was to push his two forwards wider, knocking long balls up for them to chase and then deploying the team's jack-of-all-trades, Kenny Wharton, to play in the hole just behind them. The experienced and wily head of Terry McDermott was no longer part of Charlton's plans and a more workmanlike midfield, built on the ball-winning efficiency of David McCreery, was the outcome. It meant that after the fluid attacking football that had characterised the last two years of the Cox regime, Newcastle were now little more than a kick-and-rush outfit.

To start with, though, the ploy worked like a dream, as the Magpies took to the big stage with a bang. Three straight wins marked the start of 1984-85, as Newcastle beat Leicester away, Sheffield Wednesday at home, and finally annihilated Aston Villa 3-0 at St. James' Park. At the end of the first week, United topped the table, but it couldn't last. Visits to Arsenal and Manchester United followed hard on the heels of those opening three fixtures and, from seventh heaven, the Magpies quickly found themselves within the third circle of hell. A 0-2 reverse at Highbury was followed

Sack Jack

three days later by a 0-5 roasting at Old Trafford and Newcastle United's long-expected baptism of fire was now in full swing.

The torture handed out by the Red Devils was enough to convince Charlton that several of his squad were not up to the task. John Ryan was immediately axed, replaced eventually by John Bailey from Everton. Also arriving were Gary Megson and Pat Heard from Jack's old club, Sheffield Wednesday. The new boss would continue to tinker around with the team throughout the rest of season but, at least by mid-October, the rot had been stopped. The chances of Newcastle repeating those inspirational performances at the start were never realistic, though, and so, methodically and with Big Jack placing the emphasis on tactics, United began to grind out the points necessary for their prime objective - First Division survival. The Magpies' form turned into a switchback ride of wins, draws and losses through October and *The Good, The Bad and The Ugly* became the theme as they found themselves continually making the headlines, sometimes for completely the wrong reasons.

The Good was a sublime 3-0 demolition job on Bobby Ferguson's experienced Ipswich side, an outfit bristling with internationals simply brushed aside by one of many five-star performances by Chris Waddle. The win was begun in emphatic style, as George Burley clipped an own goal over his own keeper in the first minute after Newcastle's inspirational number nine had broken away down the right wing. After that it was all one-way traffic as the black and whites continually opened up the Ipswich defence, the scoreline in the end hardly reflecting the home team's dominance.

The Bad and The Ugly followed in consecutive weeks. First, Newcastle proceeded to blow a 4-0 half-time advantage away from home at QPR. A first half

Standing in the Corner

Waddle hat-trick had helped put United into what seemed like an unassailable lead, but by the 75th minute, Rangers had reduced their deficit to 4-3. When Wharton increased the Magpies' tally to five with only minutes remaining, another QPR comeback seemed unlikely. But come back they did! Two goals in consecutive minutes made the scoreline an incredible 5-5 and even listening to events on Metro Radio was enough to induce heart palpitations. It was probably the most unbelievable First Division match of the entire decade, but Newcastle had thrown away two precious points in an inexcusable display of defensive frailty.

A week later, United were back at St. James' Park for the visit of West Ham - a fearsome grudge match which always drew the worst antics from both sets of fans. But on this occasion, it was an element of the home support that brought shame on the club. West Ham's black winger, Bobby Barnes, was repeatedly singled out throughout the game by the small contingent of delinquent lowlife that frequented the top section of the Gallowgate End. They threw bananas, made monkey chants and were generally racially abusive, the irony being that most of these white supremacist morons would have been intellectually challenged at an ant farm, let alone a zoo. The incident drew unwanted publicity onto Newcastle United and in the next home match programme, Jack Charlton and club chairman Stan Seymour both robustly condemned the perpetrators and their ideals. It underlined the fact that, as a club, Newcastle were not just paying lip service to the anti-racist message. But, as a result of a few pea-brains, it took years for the club to rid itself of the tarnished image brought about on that day.

Undaunted by the idiots, the start of 1984-85 had seen me become a more frequent visitor to St. James'

Sack Jack

Park. I was doing my A-levels at Ashington Technical College and had fallen into the company of a group of friends who were all Gallowgate End regulars. It didn't take a great deal of persuasion for them to entice me along to more of the home games and, although I still wasn't a habitual visitor to the hallowed place of worship, I was now on the second rung of the ladder. Little did I know it, but this entertaining little pastime was about to consume my soul for the duration of my adult years, in the same way that playing had in my childhood.

As the scorching summer of 1984 subsided into the frosts of November and the icy chill of December, the form that had kept Newcastle in an unlikely top half placing in Division One began also to slip away. United had only won twice in the league since that Ipswich triumph, and following a 1-3 reverse at home to Arsenal on December 29th, we were in the bottom half and very much on the slide. The next game, on New Years' Day, was the one everyone had been waiting for - Sunderland at St. James' Park, the first Tyne-Wear derby for four years. If we could win this, not only would it halt the decline, it would bring to an end four and a half years of living the unthinkable - Newcastle United being in Sunderland's shadow.

An expectant 36,500 had gathered for the big showdown, including the disagreeable sight of the Leazes End packed to overfilling with Mackems. They were also on the slide although, in the League Cup, their form had been scintillating, giving them increased hope of getting a result over us. On the day, however, there was only ever going to be one winner, even though Newcastle were lacking, through injury, our talisman, Waddle. It was Peter Beardsley however, assuming the mantle of play-maker in the absence of his strike partner, who provided the spark to set fire to and eventually sink Sunderland's ungainly ship. Pedro grabbed a hat-trick and the limelight for the first time in Division One as the Magpies vanquished the red and white enemy 3-1. And Beardsley did the business in style - his first goal was a cracker, drilled expertly through a crowd of players into the bottom corner, the second a penalty and the third a sublime one-two. Sunderland lost two players, Howard Gayle and Gary Bennett both sent off, and ended their derby match drubbing in disarray. Two months later, they lost the League Cup Final at Wembley and nine weeks after that they were relegated, but New Years' Day provided their biggest humiliation - and well they knew it. Newcastle United were back as the undisputed kings of North East football.

The Magpies' return to their rightful billing had come at a high price, however. Whilst Beardsley had been Sunderland's principal tormentor, it was Waddle who'd drawn all the plaudits for his performances up to the halfway point in the season. The so-called 'big five' clubs - Liverpool, Everton, Man. United, Arsenal and Tottenham - had all run the rule over Newcastle's prize asset and the fact that his current contract ran out in the summer of 1985 was not lost on any of them. It meant Waddle would soon become a free agent and Spurs, in particular, now showed an increasing interest in United's unsettled star. A bid on transfer deadline day made Tottenham's intentions clear and only served to compound the situation, even though it was turned down in no uncertain terms. Speculation mounted, hinting strongly at a summer move, and as the season moved into its closing stages, Waddle's form dipped, confirming to all but the most wildly optimistic fans that the Waddler was about to jump ship.

Perhaps sensing the inevitable, Charlton had made his own move as deadline day approached, snapping-up two six feet-plus through-the-middle strikers. Big

Sack Jack

Jack's first choice, George Reilly - whom Arthur Cox had tried to sign in 1983 - had apparently slipped through the net, and sensing failure at the eleventh hour, Jack turned to Manchester City and signed their black forward Tony Cunningham. No sooner was Cunningham's signature drying on the contract than Watford decided the Reilly deal was back on. Charlton, previously reticent in the transfer market, needed no further invitation and by the end of February, Newcastle boasted not one, but two of Big Jack's preferred kind of target-man striker.

The acquisition of Reilly and Cunningham prompted Jack to make another tactical switch, pulling Beardsley and Waddle deeper and wider still in his quest to provide quality balls into the middle to feed the two big men. Their first two games provided crucial home wins, 1-0 over Luton and 3-1 against Watford, a pulsating game in which both new strikers netted their first Newcastle goals. But Charlton's insistence on rigid adherence to a game plan was not going down well in certain quarters. Whilst Waddle's mind was clearly elsewhere, Peter Beardsley's form had been electric since his New Years' Day assault on Sunderland, in spite of his reservations about the new strike formation. Pedro had relished the free role he'd been given by Arthur Cox in 1983-84 but felt that the strict tactical scheming of the new boss stifled his game. He liked to be able to run at and take on defenders whenever the ball was in front of him, but on Charlton's orders, Beardsley and Waddle were meant to run into the corners, keep the ball and spoil for time whenever Newcastle had a lead. Pedro had been apt to forget from time to time, and on two occasions at 1-0, late in the Luton match, he'd run at goal in search of a second, only to lose the ball both times. Charlton did his nut! At the final whistle, Big Jack flew at Beardsley in a fit of rage, grabbing and remonstrating with the

Standing in the Corner

little striker in full view of everyone in the ground. He may well have had a point, but surely this was entirely the wrong way to deal with the situation. It appeared that Jack Charlton was about to lose Newcastle not just one star striker, but both of them.

Whilst Jack was winning the battle for points and First Division survival, he'd long since lost the confidence of his two big name players and also the goodwill of most of the fans. As the last few games of the season were played out - Newcastle finishing thirteenth on 52 points - the first chants began to be heard from the terraces. Most were not pretty, but then neither was much of the football played under Charlton in 84-85. Big Jack would argue that he'd fulfilled his brief - keeping Newcastle in the top division they'd fought so hard to get back into - but the fans demanded more. The sort of football we'd seen the previous season, making full use of our most talented players, maybe even a cup run. We'd been left wanting in all departments.

In the end, Waddle's departure for Tottenham Hotspur left an unpleasant taste - the sort of pit-of-the-stomach sickening feeling that never makes embittered fans feel any better. The fact that Waddle's transfer fee, as a free agent, was set ridiculously low by an FA tribunal was in no way Jack Charlton's fault, but that further kick in the teeth did little to help his cause with the fans. Neither did a summer of near inactivity on the incoming transfer front. Waddle, it appeared, was not going to be replaced and we faced our second season back in the top flight with a squad now two quality players down on the one we'd got promoted with.

The pre-season of 1985-86 ended with the traditional St. James' Park aperitif, the week before the first league game of the new campaign. Sheffield United, who had only recently been promoted to

Sack Jack

Division Two, provided the opposition - on the face of it, cannon fodder to supply a bit of confidence to the Newcastle players on the eve of a tricky opening month of the season. I'd made my way into Newcastle early for the game, as I was going out in town later with some mates. I had no way of knowing that this inauspicious occasion was about to become one of the defining moments in the history of Newcastle United.

The game itself was nothing to write home about, the home side depressingly unable to break down their lower division opponents. As the match panned out into a dull 1-1 stalemate, the chants that had been in evidence towards the end of the previous campaign started again; "Sack Jack, Sack Jack; Charlton must go..." and others of a more disparaging nature. There was no doubt that the perpetrators hoped their vocal assault on the manager would hit the mark, but no one expected anything would come of it. It was no worse than the things that had been shouted last season, only coming from a far sparser crowd, the ranting of a few hundred became all the more noticeable. If the board had thought anything about the fans' opinions, then Charlton, who worked without a contract, would have been out of the door in the summer. It was clear that as far as they were concerned Big Jack was in for the long haul. The final whistle blew and Jack stormed down the tunnel, not the first time he'd blown his top at the end of a match!

It was gone nine o'clock. I was in a pub on the Quayside with my mates, enjoying a drink in the company of about a dozen people - the Quayside was one of the quietest places to drink in Newcastle back then - when two young men walked in, still wearing black and white from the match. They walked straight through to the back of the pub and started talking to another group they obviously knew. All of a sudden, a raucous cheer went up, similar to that you might hear in a pub nowadays when a goal's been scored in a televised match. The cheering lasted fully twenty seconds before subsiding into one of the chants that had been aimed at Jack Charlton from the terraces a few hours earlier:

"Hello, Hello, Charlton must go, Charlton must go!"

The more people came into the pub, no doubt arriving from busier bars higher up in the city centre, the more the rumour mill kept grinding.

"Has he really gone?"

"Yes, definitely. He resigned in the tunnel straight after the match!"

It would appear it was true, then. Big Jack had quit. I had mixed feelings - in spite of his dull tactics, the loss of Waddle and the difficulties with Beardsley, I respected the bloke for what he'd achieved in football. He was a member of the same Working Men's Club as me in Ashington and was frequently seen there on Saturday nights following home games. However, it was painfully obvious that Newcastle United were going nowhere under Jack's stewardship and that change was in our best interest, even if it was at the eleventh hour.

The following morning, having kipped the night on someone's floor in Newcastle, I made my way bleary-eyed to the Haymarket to catch a bus home to Morpeth. The *Sunday Sun's* headline confirmed the rumours: "JACK QUITS". I bought a copy for the bus journey and immediately turned to the back page. "So who will be next?" asked the Sports Editor. His reporters had done a tour of the bars as the news was breaking and everyone had a favourite - Malcolm Macdonald from Huddersfield, Frank Clark from Orient, bring back Arthur Cox. The list of ex-Newcastle stars lined up to take over was endless.

One name, however, an ex-teammate of both Macdonald and Clark, who was already at the club as

Sack Jack

first team coach, was never mentioned. It was hardly surprising - since his quiet exit from first team action in 1975, this stalwart had given continuous service to Newcastle United on the coaching staff, albeit in an extremely low-profile capacity. Many fans could have been forgiven for not even realising he was still there. Nonetheless, given the shortage of time to the start of the new season, it was to that man, former goalkeeper Iam McFaul, that the board of directors turned in their hour of need. McFaul was given the manager's hotseat on a caretaker basis until a suitable replacement for Charlton could be found. And hot it was indeed! Newcastle, unable to beat Sheffield United at home, were due to face Liverpool at home, and Manchester United, Tottenham and Arsenal, all away, before the end of September. If there was ever a time an uninitiated rookie manager faced real pressure, this was it. If he wanted the job full-time, Iam McFaul's hour of reckoning was nigh!

Four

Iam McFaul's
Black & White Army

My journey to Newcastle on matchday was always made in the same way, afternoon or evening kick-off. Local train from Morpeth to Newcastle Central, then a walk around the back of Blackfriars and along Stowell Street to come out on Gallowgate next to the coach station. It was the same mode of transport on the way back, the 5.15 Berwick train on Saturdays or the 10.45 to Morpeth on Wednesday night, which in the days of 7.30 kick-offs allowed me an hour in the Labour Club after the game. Ah, bliss!

I'd now been residing in Morpeth for 11 years, and in 1985 I was still living at home with my parents, hoping in vain to find some white-collar employment locally following my A-levels. I'd drifted into watching Newcastle play up to that point, still unable to call myself a regular at St. James' Park or ever having been to see an away game. But things had been changing gradually over the last twelve months and in 1985-86, my career as a football supporter was about to take off. So on that Wednesday evening, a week and a half after Charlton resigned, I was breaking new ground again by going to see the first home game of the season for only the second time, against unfashionable Luton Town.

Far from the glamour of Keegan's debut three years before, this was seen as a low-key curtain-raiser by many fans, especially as Division One aristocrats Liverpool were the visitors on the coming Saturday.

Iam McFaul's Black & White Army

Nevertheless, a crowd of 21,933 diehards was present, expecting due reward with the scalp of the Hatters. Luton hadn't read the script! Before too long the away side had carved out a two goal advantage and, but for the heroics of Newcastle keeper Martin Thomas, it would've been three courtesy of a penalty save early in the second half. Newcastle gained their second wind, and by 80 minutes the scores were level through strikes from Glenn Roeder and Beardsley. The last ten minutes saw a mad scramble for the winner but it never came, Newcastle having left themselves too much to do in going two goals down.

After the match, a stone's throw from the ground, the spacious bar of the Labour Club soon filled up, with the wise sages of Gallowgate holding congress on the events they'd just witnessed. I found myself tuning in to their conversations while I was supposed to be listening to the idle teenage tittle-tattle of my mates. For a novice like myself, the thoughts of blokes who'd put in maybe twenty years on the terraces of St. James' were always worth listening to. The post-match beer alone made the visit to the club worthwhile, but the knowledge gained from eavesdropping on those wiser than myself was invaluable to my credibility as I began to mix in more committed circles in the year ahead.

McFaul wasted no time in discarding Big Jack's route-one tactics, but he still lacked the embarrassment of riches once possessed by Arthur Cox. As Beardsley was the only regular first-team player completely confident with the ball at his feet, a fluent passing game was never going to be a luxury Newcastle could afford in the unforgiving environment of Division One. So, Plan B was hatched: they would keep the ball on the deck as often as possible and only give it some welly when no other option was open. Peter Beardsley was the obvious jewel in the Magpies' crown now that Waddle was gone, and in a chalk and cheese strike partnership, he was paired with the gangling George 'Rambo' Reilly up front for the early part of 1985-86. The rest of the squad often had to be chopped and changed on a match-to-match basis. Apart from McCreery, the midfield consisted of newly-acquired wide-man Ian Stewart as well as the club's youngest-ever player, Neil McDonald. Then there was Paul Gascoigne. He broke into the first team at the start of that season with the sort of panache that would become his trademark. Gazza had captained Newcastle's youngsters to FA Youth Cup success at the close of the previous campaign, a season that started with Jack Charlton wanting to sack him for his disruptive behaviour! According to legend, it was Iam McFaul who talked Charlton out of it and the achievement of both men in moulding the young scamp into an exciting prospect was soon to be appreciated by the St. James' Park faithful. The utility players were John Anderson and Kenny Wharton, each able to play in midfield or as full-backs paired together, or with left-back John Bailey. Ever-present centre halves Jeff Clarke and Glenn Roeder, the club captain, completed the back line along with goalkeeper Martin Thomas.

After drawing the first two matches, Newcastle then went and beat mighty Liverpool, the only goal of the game bundled into the net by Reilly with only five minutes remaining. By the end of September we were fourth, having won four games more, lost two - away at Man. United and Spurs - and gained a highly respectable draw at Arsenal. Progress had also been made into the third round of the League Cup and the board was suitably impressed, giving McFaul the manager's job full-time until the end of the season. Once again, our form became erratic through October. The Magpies won twice away and lost twice at home and although winning ways were eventually re-established at St. James', a tempestuous game took place with Graham Taylor's Watford first, leaving most who were there with a horrible feeling of déjà vu.

The atmosphere at home games in those roofless Gallowgate End days always seemed to come to a head after the clocks went back and the last half hour of the game had to be played under floodlights. The Gallowgate End was split into three sections, with the ones in the centre and the easternmost side locked in a fierce rivalry. You had to be either a man of 'The Scoreboard' or a man of 'The Corner' (I belonged to the latter faction) and mutual insults in the form of chants like "Why's the Scoreboard Full of S**t?" and vice versa frequently livened-up quiet passages of play. On the day of the Watford game, however, the derision of the entire Gallowgate End was to be reserved for just one man, a figure of previous notoriety on Tyneside and soon to be one of still greater infamy.

The Trent House was packed to the rafters for the ritual of the pre-match drink. Amid the cacophony of noise, it was just possible for me to tune in, as usual, to the conversations around me on the prospects for the match to come.

"We've got to win today," insisted a voice over by the bar, through a haze of smoke, "we need to get the momentum back after the last two home games."

"Nee chance of that today, marra," replied the bloke next to him, pointing to the back page of his programme. "Seen who the ref is? Trelford F***ing Mills!"

There was a collective groan all round the bar. Trelford Mills was no friend of the Toon Army. In 1983, he'd taken it upon himself to disallow two Newcastle goals in the last five minutes of a cup replay against Brighton. TV highlights later confirmed the fans' belief that both goals should have stood but Brighton had still won 1-0! Most Geordies hoped they'd seen the last of Mr. Mills, but here he was back again for the first time in almost three years.

Not that Newcastle fans had anything to complain about in the first half. Watford took a deserved lead and held onto it despite the Barnsley referee's only howler, a mistake to the benefit of the home side. After a clear foul on Beardsley inside the box, Mills allowed the advantage when the ball broke kindly for Tony Cunningham. Only after the black striker had smashed his shot against the bar and over did the ref point to the spot, dismissing Watford's protests. Beardsley squandered the opportunity though, and the 21,000 inside St. James' Park looked to the heavens.

Despite a lacklustre performance from the rest of the side, Gascoigne had started to look increasingly dangerous after the break and a Newcastle equaliser still, somehow, seemed on the cards. Sure enough, on 80 minutes Gazza unleashed a ferocious drive, which flew straight into the top corner of the goal at the Gallowgate End. The relief was palpable all around the stadium and, roared on by a crowd now nearing fever pitch, Newcastle surged forward in search of a winner.

With a minute remaining, Gascoigne swung over a cross from the right, which cleared both central defenders and broke for George Reilly as he stole away, unmarked at the far post. Reilly lunged forward to meet the ball and powered a diving header high into the far corner of the net. The Gallowgate End went berserk. Crowd surges spilled down the terraces and the din must have been heard clearly right across the city! Then the celebrations were stifled in mid-cry. No, not again, surely he couldn't... He could, Mills had disallowed the goal. But why? There'd been no flag. Reilly and all the other Newcastle players attacking the cross were clearly onside! The referee began to indicate that the decision was for pushing and, as black and white shirts closed-in to protest, pointed to the 'goalscorer' as the guilty party. What? Rambo had been in so much space he'd have had time to light a cigar and take a nip of whisky before sticking the chance away! It was a diabolical decision and though Newcastle hardly deserved all three points, Trelford Mills had done it again, denying United another victory at the death!

Suddenly, the Gallowgate End had been transformed from a state of euphoria to one of furious outrage. Grown men hammered their fists against the steel perimeter fence in anger, as the besieged referee attempted to restore order for the resultant free kick to be taken. Stewards and police moved in to prevent any incursion onto the playing area. Inevitably, one incensed spectator made it past the cordon, racing out towards Mills from the unfenced East Stand Paddock before being bundled to the ground by an alert steward. The game was quickly over, 1-1, but the black and white army was incandescent and a large crowd gathered afterwards outside the West Stand, refusing to let the matter rest. In the end the referee had to be given a police escort down the A1 as far as Scotch Corner! The only consolation for the irate supporters, as the motorcade sped away towards the Tyne Bridge, was the fact he didn't referee Newcastle matches every week.

It was just as well, as by now I'd attended all ten home games so far that season. But even without the hardship of Trelford Mills' presence, St. James' Park was hardly a place of great comfort for the regular fan. Back in 1985, Newcastle United's home ground was a million miles removed from the present day super-stadium. In the mid-Eighties, it wasn't just the club's inability to win trophies that was derided by supporters of other football clubs. Under-ambition, manifest in the way we failed to compete in the transfer market and, above all, the wretched condition of the ground, were uppermost in the jibes of our rivals. The only vaguely impressive part of St. James' Park was the East Stand, built in the 1970s and the only structure that still remains. Opposite, the West Stand dated back to the early 1900s. This was a crumbling relic made out of wood and corrugated iron, and was hopelessly outdated with its future in doubt on safety grounds following the recent fire at Bradford City. The rest of the stadium, the Gallowgate & Leazes Ends and the paddock situated in front of the West Stand, was all uncovered terracing. This meant that standing punters always got piss wet-through whenever it rained. When it snowed, however, as it had in the week running up to the next home game with Southampton, St. James' Park became a winter wonderland for the fans.

The day before the game, the club had enlisted an army of helpers to clear snow off the pitch and terraces so the match could go ahead. The by-product was mounds of snow that had been shovelled into the gully right at the front of the terracing. Some entrepreneur, in the true spirit of Thatcherite free enterprise, had arrived early on matchday and made hundreds of snowballs, which he packed into plastic bags and buried back in the snow. At half-time, he collected his wares and went round the Corner and the Scoreboard selling snowballs at 5p a time. The outcome was a massive snowball fight between the rival Gallowgate End factions! Some even turned on the peacekeeping force. A young lad high up in the Scoreboard managed a direct hit on a policeman's helmet as he stood by the side of the pitch. The scallywag raised his arms to take the acclaim of the whole Gallowgate End and was promptly nicked by another officer standing right behind him on the terraces!

Iam McFaul's Black & White Army

Such winter revelry was mirrored by Newcastle's performance on the pitch. Having taken an early lead through Roeder, we'd allowed Southampton to equalise and more valuable home points looked like slipping away. It was into the last quarter of an hour when a clever ball from debutant Paul Stephenson found Beardsley sprinting down the inside-left channel. Forced wide by the attentions of Mark Wright, Pedro managed to squeeze a shot from an acute angle just inside the far post. Once again, the Gallowgate End celebrated in its inimitable fashion, and as Wright and Peter Shilton held a solemn debate about just how the ball ended up in their net, yet more snow rained down from the terraces to compound their misery!

The Christmas programme came and went, bestowing mixed fortunes on the inconsistent Magpies. Four points from four drawn games was the return, one at home and three away. Not bad, especially considering that two were the return against Liverpool and and a home game with reigning champions Everton. The Everton game at St. James' was a pulsating New Year's Day encounter that ended 2-2, Newcastle having led for much of the second half. A few days later, United were inexplicably dumped out of the FA Cup, 2-0 at home by lowly Second Division Brighton, this time without any assistance from the referee! Even a hot date in Morpeth later that Saturday couldn't raise my spirits; the poor girl had to spend the evening listening to my complaints about the match. Romance, unsurprisingly, didn't blossom and Newcastle too would have to fare without the romance of the FA Cup for at least another year!

As the season wore on, so did the duration of my unemployment. My best chance had been the previous autumn's civil service intake, for which I'd been short-listed, interviewed and then reserve listed. It had now been three months, though, and I'd still heard nothing.

Standing in the Corner

With few other opportunities arising, I began to think seriously about moving into full-time higher education in the next academic year. It would be a big move, however, and one that required careful consideration. So I decided that by visiting a couple of old school friends who were both already at university I would get a taste of what student life was really like. It just so happened that they attended colleges in the vicinity of Newcastle's next two away games at QPR and Nottingham Forest.

Away travel was an all-new experience for me and, for starters, there would be no bigger baptism of fire than a game in 'the smoke'. I travelled down to London by coach on the Friday and out to where my mate studied, Brunel University in Uxbridge, by tube. I still had much to learn about life away from the dole queues of the North East and the meticulously planned Friday night out turned into a cataclysmic two-way culture shock. One of my mate's neighbours in their 'concrete city' halls of residence had a car and we travelled west, out of London, to the leafy Buckinghamshire commuter town of Beaconsfield. The car park outside the first pub we visited looked like the players' equivalent of the one behind the West Stand at St. James' Park. Nowhere else in the North East could you have found such a collection of expensive brand new cars in one place. But in the Home Counties, such places were common, as Thatcherism brought unprecedented prosperity to the South of England. There was everything from Porsches down to customised XR3i's and inside the bar, not a single punter was over the age of 21. There was probably more wealth in that one establishment than in the whole city centre of Newcastle on a Saturday night. They were yuppies of course, I'd heard all about them; unqualified in the main but upwardly mobile, as long as the place they earned all their dosh was only thirty-odd miles from home. B*****ds! Whilst their shameless riches were a real eye-opener to a mere northern Dole Waller, their impression of me seemed to be that I was something from another planet. The last eighteen months, which I'd spent almost exclusively on the Gallowgate End, had turned me into a living example of a 1980s travelling Mag - even though this was only my first away trip! But to a crowd of yuppies, my attire must have made me look like a being from another world. The silver-grey pinstripe away shirt I was wearing really did look like part of a space suit and my unrecognisable South-East Northumberland accent probably sounded to them like an alien tongue. The way they all parted like the Red Sea as I walked past them to the bar suggested they really did think I was extra-terrestrial. But in hindsight they were probably thinking, "Which one of us is the Geordie football hooligan going to hit first?!!"

The journey through the capital on that Friday evening had proved to be useful reconnaissance, as there would be no easy route back from Uxbridge to Loftus Road the next day. I had to re-trace my steps into Central London and then go back out to Shepherd's Bush; a trip involving four separate tube rides. Once there, I discovered that Loftus Road was a compact, modern ground, most unlike St. James' Park, and although its capacity was less than 30,000, the fact it was completely covered made the noise from the travelling Newcastle supporters sound all the more impressive. In those days, the repertoire of songs sung by the Toon Army at home games was far greater than it is today, but at QPR the three thousand black and white followers performed a set far more extensive than anything I'd heard previously. There were songs from the seventies and songs from the early eighties, all driven along by the backbeat of three thousand pairs of feet hammering on the upper tier of the away terrace.

Standing in the Corner

Sadly, the performance of the Magpies failed to live up to the vocal encouragement of the fans and the game itself was never going to compare with the one there the previous season, which had ended 5-5. In the finish, QPR, starting a few places below us in the table, ran out 3-1 winners, aided in no small part by their artificial pitch but also, crucially, by a much greater hunger for the points. Newcastle slipped to 11th place in the table and we held onto our record of not having dropped into the bottom half that season only by virtue of goal difference. Another piss-up, surrounded by rugby fans in a crumby student bar in Twickenham, was scant consolation but, the next weekend, amends were made in the form of a 3-2 home win over Coventry. A week later, I was on my way to the City Ground and the next away game at Forest.

As I set out on my journey to Nottingham from the Central Station, snow was just beginning to fall on Tyneside. The weatherfront carrying it was moving up from the south and apparently there'd been an overnight fall of a couple of inches in the Midlands. The hundred or so black and whites travelling on that train were all well aware that the reason for our journey hinged entirely on a pitch inspection being made at 11 o'clock. The further south we travelled, the more ominously deep the white stuff grew. I was going to visit a mate anyway, so my journey wouldn't have been wasted, but I was still desperate to see the game. It wasn't until we were well past Leeds that someone with a radio managed to pick up an East Midlands station and got the news we were all praying for. The match was on!

Inside the City Ground, it was difficult to understand why the game hadn't been called off. The side of the pitch nearest to the huge main stand was fine; the morning sun had completely thawed it. But on the other side, the grass shaded by the smaller stand opposite was still frostbound and an inch of snow ran the length of the park. These icy remains would certainly make play difficult but would they favour us and hinder Brian Clough's more skilful side? The match opened with both sides struggling to cope.

The conditions did prove almost unplayable but it still took two moments of breathtaking individual skill from Peter Beardsley to secure an unexpected 2-1 victory for the Magpies. McFaul had restored the little man's free role and the response had been awesome. His electrifying form had already aroused the interest of England manager Bobby Robson, surely now his call-up into the full international squad was inevitable. As we celebrated Pedro's second goal, a typical mazy run and surgical finish, a crowd surge took me past a mate from Morpeth, whom I hadn't known was going to Forest.

"Alright, Pete!" shouted Keith as I bounced past him down the steep terrace. Keith, who I knew better by his nickname Oges, was one of my two principal Gallowgate End pals that I always stood with on the terraces at home games. He, the other lad Paul from Ashington, and I had made a point that season of meeting up outside St. James' Park before each game. It meant that whether or not there was someone I knew on the platform at Morpeth station, I wouldn't be standing in the middle of a crowd of strangers at the match. Oges would soon become my best mate in football circles as we racked up the miles, not to mention the pints, travelling to hundreds of matches together over the ensuing years.

From the springboard of those two wins, Newcastle went on a run of five consecutive victories that took us to within a few points of a top six placing with only ten games left. It was a lofty position for a Newcastle side that had, without Waddle, been expected to struggle. Now it was time for 'the Waddler' to make his first comeback to St. James' since his departure the previous summer. Ironically, as his new team Spurs prepared to make the journey up to Tyneside on 22nd March 1986, it was Newcastle that was the higher placed club in the league. Tottenham's early season form had faded and they were now sitting in mid-table. The Geordie faithful, all 31,000, were standing by for Chris Waddle to be taught a lesson!

Everyone at St. James' Park expected Waddle to be given a rough ride. In fact, most were prepared to assist and as soon as the mulleted Leam Lane exile appeared for the warm-up, a chorus of boos rolled down the terraces and even emanated from the more reserved people of the stands. "Judas, Judas," roared the crowd, as Waddle hastily headed for the sanctuary of the changing room. Spurs started brightly, their legion of stars shining over Newcastle's more modest outfit, and they deservedly opened the scoring with less than twenty minutes played. Newcastle would not be overawed though, and back we came. Billy Whitehurst, signed in November to replace George Reilly, drilled an equaliser into the bottom right hand corner at the Gallowgate End and before half-time John Anderson fired us into a 2-1 lead. The chants coming from the terraces were now of a far more unkind and personal nature and a lesser man than Chris Waddle might have asked to be taken off at half-time. No such luck! Within a minute of the restart Waddle headed a soft equaliser for Spurs and milked his opportunity to celebrate in front of his principal tormentors in the Gallowgate End.

The match ended 2-2 and with the end of Newcastle's winning run came a spell of rollercoaster form. We weren't able to string together two wins, two draws or two defeats for the rest of the campaign. There were highs - the 4-1 thumping of fifth place Sheffield Wednesday at home on Easter Monday - and lows - a 1-8 defeat by West Ham at Upton Park in which Newcastle fielded three different goalkeepers! Trelford Mills returned to St. James' Park and was struck by a half-eaten pie hurled from the Gallowgate End after he'd allowed Man. United an offside goal and awarded them a dubious penalty in the first five minutes. The Red Devils won the meaningless midweek encounter 4-2, but Mills' performance was of more lasting significance. He'd just set the blueprint for the refereeing of Manchester United fixtures in the 1990s!

By the time I went to Filbert Street to see the final game of the season, Newcastle had slipped to tenth in the table. But, a win at Leicester could still see us bounce all the way back up to eighth. Accompanied by fellow Gallowgate Ender Paul, we were making a trip planned weeks earlier intended to celebrate a top-six finish and Peter Beardsley's inclusion into the England squad for the World Cup Finals in Mexico. The top six bit would have to wait! After an uneventful first period, Glenn Roeder got into the thick of the action straight after the interval, brilliantly parrying an Alan Smith effort to deny Leicester. Keeper Dave McKellar, on loan from Carlisle, was less successful with the resultant penalty and the Foxes ran out 2-0 winners, avoiding relegation at the eleventh hour.

Midway through the second half, a rumour started running like wildfire among the away supporters. Apparently, Second Division results were such that struggling Sunderland stood in imminent peril of relegation to Division Three! Celebrations erupted as a carnival atmosphere descended on Filbert Street. The reserved home fans were bemused by the commotion but sadly the news of the Mackems' demise was twelve months premature. Our result meant that we slipped a further place to eleventh, being leap-frogged by Spurs. Nonetheless, by Newcastle's mid-eighties standards it had been a good season. Iam McFaul was elevated to hero status by the fans, and after his heroics for England in Mexico, Peter Beardsley became a God! Times were good on Tyneside, for the summer of 1986 at least.

Five

Lies, Damn Lies and Statistics

Newcastle United were watched by an average of 23,432 fans in the twenty-one First Division games played at St. James' Park in 1985-86, my first "full" season as a regular fan. Such statistics may be of little interest to some; they'll probably be purely academic to the modern day Sky Sports armchair fan armed with the knowledge that this amounts to less than half the attendances regularly seen at Newcastle today. To the committed Newcastle United supporter of a certain age however, such details are almost as important as the results, the points total and the final league placing itself.

One of the favourite modern chants directed at Newcastle fans by opposition supporters of a contingent of 'large clubs' goes:

Where were you when you were shit?
Where were you - when - you - were - shit?

It's a song based on the belief by followers of sides like Everton and Manchester City, clubs once way ahead of Newcastle but now far smaller in terms of results and attendances, that the Toon Army at St James' used to number, both for individual matches and on average, well under 10,000. They're completely wrong on both counts. For the record, Newcastle's

Standing in the Corner

lowest average home gate, 16,273, was in the austere days when Cox replaced McGarry as manager in 1980-81 and, although attendances have dropped below five figures on the odd occasion, those matches remain a rarity in the club's history.

To take into serious consideration what average attendances from seasons almost twenty years apart represent, it is necessary to take into account factors like the size of crowds at football matches across the board. In the 1980s, gates at all top-flight clubs were significantly less than those of today. Take Manchester United, for example. In 1985-86 their league average was just over 40,000, today it's closer to 70,000. That's an even bigger difference than Newcastle's average in 1986 as opposed to 51,922 in 2003 and no-one's accusing Man. United fans of being part-time supporters!

What is hard to accept, though, isn't the ignorance of our detractors but the hypocrisy. In 1983-84 Newcastle, promoted to the top flight as third placed team in Division Two, averaged 29,834 at home. Meanwhile, in the same season, Everton, who finished mid-table in Division One, won the FA Cup and reached the League Cup final, averaged just 19,343 at Goodison Park. Hold on a minute, surely that can't be right! The Toffees, the loyalest football supporters in the world, averaging less than 20,000 and over 10,000 down on Newcastle United when we were s**t? I'm afraid it is; you see, their excuse was that Everton were having a miserable season until a mistimed back-pass by Kevin Brock, then of Oxford United, gifted them a goal in a League Cup Quarter-Final, thereby resurrecting their season. Most of the league games at Goodison had been played by then. Oh, all right then, I knew there had to be a perfectly reasonable explanation!

The next season, the average attendance at Everton rocketed to 32,000. Why the sudden increase? They

Lies, Damn Lies and Statistics

won the League Championship for the first time in almost twenty years, of course, banishing the memory of a decade of Division One mediocrity that had led to the slide in their gates. The question has to be asked as to where those missing 13,000 Toffees were when they were 'shit' in the season immediately prior to the return of the Championship to Goodison Park? There was no two-decade interval in which for trends in football attendances to rise. The truth is of course that Everton too have that fickle element in their fanbase that is evident at all football clubs when fortunes are at a low ebb. And just how low is low? How favourably does 19,343 for a club that finished mid-table in the top flight and won the FA Cup compare with 16,273 for one that achieved only eleventh place in Division Two?

Manchester City fans are equally self-righteous and deluded, believing that their average home gates never fell to embarrassing lows during that period of bread and water in English league football. Incorrect! From a high of 40,000 in 1976, the year they beat flu-ravaged Newcastle in the League Cup Final, City's average at Maine Road had slumped to less than half that a decade later. True, their status had fallen from that of a top-six Division One outfit to a yo-yo club between the top two divisions but that sort of thing, apparently, didn't matter to the loyal Blue Moon Army! Didn't it? Back then, according to the City faithful, only fickle supporters like those of Newcastle United failed to get to home midweek cup-ties in insufficient numbers to muster less than a 10,000 gate. Not so! In early October 1986, a pathetic 9,373 saw City's League Cup Second Round, Second Leg at home to Southend, a tie in which there was everything to play for at 0-0 after the first engagement.

If you were to believe the patter-merchants of clubs like Everton and City you'd have to conclude that Newcastle United fans were unique in their failure to turn up when the chips were down. On the contrary, when you take a closer look at the actual figures, it's plain to see that someone is talking out of their arse! 1985-86 may have been my first season as a regular, but I'd already been around long enough to recall now that such pathetic claims are tripe. Next time they start that chant at St. James', just remember that we're as entitled to sing it as them!

Six

Survival

The beginning of 1986-87 was a time of great change. The sublime blue star disappeared from the front of Newcastle United's famous black and white shirts, replaced by a brand no one in the North East had even heard of. If ever a sponsorship deal seemed like family ties, it was Newcastle United and Scottish and Newcastle Breweries. The fact that the grand old Tyne Brewery cast its fatherly gaze across Barrack Road and over the old West Stand only added to the feeling they were meant to be together. What was even more significant was that the majority of Newcastle supporters consumed their sponsor's products and regarded the company logo almost as much as a badge of local pride as the black and white stripes themselves! S&N's replacement as club sponsor was the Warrington-based brewing firm Greenall-Whitley. Who? I later discovered that in Greenalls' hinterland of the North West, drinkers gave their beer the nickname 'Piddley-Diddley'. To add insult to injury, in covering up the old sponsorship slogans a complete mess was made of the scoreboard, making the already decrepit unit look like something recovered from the council recycling depot!

I too had a change of sponsor - Northumberland Education Authority took over from the D.H.S.S.! I'd quit the dole-queue and become a full-time student, relocating to Preston to begin a three-year course at Lancashire Polytechnic. Following Newcastle could well have been difficult, cast adrift 130 miles from Tyneside with no transport of my own but, luckily, help was at hand.

Newcastle had begun the new season in poor form. A not altogether unexpected 0-2 home defeat by Liverpool was followed by two creditable draws at Luton and Spurs. After that, our form slumped and by the time I'd embarked on student life at the beginning of October, Newcastle were plumb bottom of Division One and already out of the League Cup. It was a slow agonising torture for the fans as we watched our team lose the first three home games in a row, and even when we'd clawed back a 0-2 deficit against Sheffield Wednesday, equalising in the last minute, we still managed to concede again in injury time.

Attendances at St. James' Park surprisingly remained stable - far from falling away as those opposition fans would have you believe! Averaging just fewer than 25,000, it meant that crowd advantage remained a vital factor at home, eventually telling as the team finally put some more points on the board with a crucial win over Man. City. Then Wimbledon, playing Newcastle for the first time ever, were undone by an audacious strike from Paul Gascoigne. Even better, I was there to see both games and, in addition, almost every home and away match Newcastle played from early October until the third week in December.

Fortune had smiled on me: Oges - have car, will go to Newcastle games home and away - was now also living in Preston, not as a student but working for Midland Bank at a branch near Blackpool. And it wasn't long before I discovered another Toon fan wandering about the Lancs. Poly. Campus. Raj, an Asian lad from Newcastle, was also a Gallowgate End regular in need of a lift to the match. Without much more than a brief introduction, he too was press-ganged into the hastily assembled Preston branch of the travelling Toon Army. I made many other new friends in the generous 'Freshers' Fortnight' that was provided at my new place of study, a two week festival of drinking, sleeping and more drinking. Many, as you might expect, were also football fans, followers of rival clubs like Sheffield United, Derby and Liverpool but, unlike us, they lacked the will to get out to support their teams on a regular basis. Attitudes were different then, when being a full-on football supporter often saw you categorised as no better than a thug! Especially by some of the politically correct types all too often found on the campus of a 1980s Higher Education establishment. The thing that set Oges, Raj and me apart from practically all the students with whom we mixed was the fact that we were almost never seen in Preston on Saturday afternoons! Instead we went on the road in that first college term as the Toon at last started to get results that suggested they might, just might turn the corner and get out of trouble.

In the first away game we saw, though, Newcastle proceeded to throw away the initiative we'd gained from those two home wins, going-down 2-0 at Villa Park. Aston Villa's want-away England midfielder, Steve Hodge, was not intent on doing what one of today's overpaid prima donnas might in going AWOL or under-performing. Exactly the opposite, he was selling himself with an outstanding performance, on the day outclassing opposite number Peter Beardsley, and scoring both goals. By the final whistle we'd been treated to almost 75 minutes of "You're Going Down with the City" and been made aware not once, but twice that Steve Hodge drove a Montego by the Holte End scoreboard. Well at least they had one that worked! Newcastle were back in bottom spot, so much for the revival.

Standing in the Corner

Two weeks and a dull home draw later, there was a swift return for me to Leicester City. They hadn't managed to raise their fortunes much since my last visit on the previous season's final day and were back in the mire just a few places above us. Another six-pointer, or so it was billed. "Attack, Attack, Attack-Attack-Attack," pleaded the Toon Army as our team just seemed intent on settling for an away point against the lacklustre Filbert Street men. Newcastle had led and been pegged back early in the contest, and as the game fizzled out into a dour 1-1 draw, the only suggestion of further entertainment followed an untidy challenge by Osman on Kenny Wharton, right in front of the travelling faithful. Raj, who fancied himself as a bit of a hooligan, was incensed and stomped off purposefully down the terracing towards the resulting fracas, setting fire to his programme as he went. A sudden flurry of activity from the alarmed stewards, not to mention the presence of an eight-foot-high perimeter fence round the pitch, persuaded Raj to think better of his actions. The programme hadn't been a good choice of weapon anyway - it was reduced to cinders in seconds, and the miscreant returned to his place, fingers singed for his troubles! In the end, the point we'd earned wasn't enough to get us out of bottom spot. Taken in context the result suggested better times ahead, but in the short term a 2-2 draw against Watford meant it was business as usual the following week with two more home points squandered.

The first turning point of the season came at Chelsea. It wasn't THE turning point - that came much later - but it heralded a series of good performances and a consequent haul of points, which would prove invaluable at the season's end. Newcastle's form at Stamford Bridge has never been good. We'd been knocked-off top spot there by four to nil in the promotion season and hadn't won either of the two subsequent top-flight fixtures. Results there ever since have been lamentable, but on that day, 22nd November 1986, Newcastle claimed that rarest of collectors' items - a win at Stamford Bridge - and oh what fun it was to see United win away!

The Bridge, in those days, was as much of a run-down dump as the contemporary St. James' Park. There was one new stand, one old wooden stand and open terracing at both ends, interrupted only over a small section high on the home terraces by "the Shed". Worse still, the ground was oval, which meant that standing on the away end you were a quarter of a mile, at the closest, from the nearest goal and the other end of the pitch was just visible, through binoculars, on the horizon!

Andy Thomas, who'd only recently been signed by Newcastle, was about to enjoy a brief period of outstanding goalscoring form. He got two that day and Peter Beardsley the other in our 3-1 victory. Pedro hadn't been turning in the regular world-class performances that got him to the World Cup in the previous campaign, one of the main reasons for United's hitherto poor league showing. Now though, that form was once again beginning to glimmer and that afternoon he ran rings round the Chelsea midfield and back four alike.

Ken Bates would no doubt have been fuming, but that was Blues' boss John Hollins' problem. Our problem was how to get back to Oges' car in one piece, without running into any pissed-off Chelsea hooligans on the way. We'd already endured one scrape with the locals that afternoon - Oges having collided with a lunatic cockney driver on Hangar Lane Roundabout - and as a consequence of the delay that caused, we were parked the best part of a mile away from the ground. It was well off the main Fulham Broadway and in the opposite direction to the heavy police escort afforded to the rest of the travelling contingent. We had to pick our way through a dimly-lit warren of streets praying we wouldn't run into any home fans. Raj fancied that we could 'take them' and, much to Oges and my annoyance, kept singing his hooligan ditties all the way back. Chelsea possessed some of the most notoriously violent thugs in football in the eighties and God knows what might have happened if we'd met any that evening. Raj nearly ended up getting killed - by us! Deep down, although he could be a prat, I think even he was relieved when we made it back to the car without incident and the long journey home could at last be one to savour.

The following week, Andy Thomas was at it again, scoring twice as resurgent Newcastle hammered West Ham 4-0 at St. James' Park. The goalfest was broadcast live on Sunday afternoon TV and, as well as three more points, it gave Newcastle back a lot of lost credibility. West Ham had been surprise title contenders the previous season and, of course, had beaten us 8-1 at Upton Park. Even after their four-goal mauling, the Hammers still sat comfortably in the top six. It showed just what an in-form United were capable of. Thomas wasn't finished there either. The following Wednesday night saw the three of us making the short journey from Preston to Goodison Park for a Full Member's Cup tie. Everton had a magnificent side. Recent winners of that crowd-boosting League Championship, as well as the FA Cup and Cup Winners' Cup, they'd managed to appear at Wembley seven times in the previous three seasons. Howard Kendall seemed keen to make it eight in four, because he fielded an almost full-strength team for what ranked only as a Mickey Mouse competition. Everton were 4-0 up inside 25 minutes, running-out 5-2 winners after they eased off following the fourth, with Andy Thomas the scorer of both Newcastle goals.

Survival

Thomas' remarkable goal return was all the more amazing as Iam McFaul had just doubled the Newcastle transfer record by at last signing a quality strike partner for Peter Beardsley. Billy Whitehurst, who was at best a second division striker, had been shown the door early in the season. Andy Thomas had come the other way in a deal with Oxford, but it was former England and West Ham centre forward Paul Goddard, who'd cost a record £415,000, of whom great things were expected. Goddard started repaying the fee in earnest in the next game at Charlton Athletic.

This time, Raj and I were making the journey south without the assistance of Oges, taking advantage of a £5 coach trip to the capital, organised for a student demo. Charlton had a lively young team - including a youthful Robert Lee - which had gained promotion the previous season in spite of financial difficulties and an ongoing ground-share arrangement with Crystal Palace. In his programme notes, Charlton boss Lennie Lawrence warned that Newcastle must be given due respect after the previous weekend's demolition of West Ham. His team obviously hadn't read them, Rob Lee and co hammering away at our defence and inevitably opening the scoring early in the second half. Was the recent run of form about to end in disappointment? Not if Paul Goddard had anything to do with it. By the hour mark, Newcastle, kicking towards the away fans, were getting back into the game and a ball from Beardsley found Goddard lurking on the edge of the Charlton box. He held off the challenge of centre-half Shirtliff and drilled the ball past Bob Boulder into the bottom corner, 1-1. It was the first of his many crucial goals that season and sent the travelling faithful, 4.000-strong, into seasonal raptures. The good form continued the following week with another home victory over top-six opposition, this time Forest beaten 3-2 and Andy Thomas on target yet again. It was now mid-December and we were at last starting to climb the table away from trouble, but if the Toon Army thought we were now cruising towards a second successive top-half finish, we were in for a rude awakening. This season was destined to be a rollercoaster ride all the way to its final weeks and poor form was about to return with immediate effect.

Newcastle proceeded to lose the next six league games in a row in a depressing festive programme, the only fortunate thing for me being that I only saw one of the away games, a 0-2 defeat at Anfield. There really was no benefit in this, as the home results were just as depressing, a 0-4 Boxing Day drubbing by Everton followed by a 1-2 defeat at the hands of Coventry. The miserable sequence was finally broken by a 2-2 draw with Luton at St. James' Park, but even this game ended with us all tearing our hair out. Goddard, clean through with only the keeper to beat in the final minute, had the ball taken off his toes as he prepared to shoot, but not by a defender. His strike partner for the day, Tony Cunningham, had decided to take the chance on himself but only succeeded in running the ball harmlessly out for a goal kick. The following week we lost 1-2 at QPR. Taking just one point from a possible 24, needless to say, dumped us unceremoniously back to the bottom of Division One, staring relegation squarely in the face!

One minor crumb of comfort for the faithful in this dismal period of league form was an FA Cup run to the fifth round, the first time in five seasons we'd got past the first hurdle. The run was achieved, it has to be admitted, through two slender home victories over Fourth Division opponents. Those two sides - Northampton and Preston North End - were, however, the eventual champions & runners-up of that division and as such comprised potentially embarrassing banana skins for a senior club in Newcastle's precarious position. The Preston game was, of course, a plum draw for Oges, Raj and myself, and we spent the week before the match goading the Lillywhite supporters in the Preston pubs we frequented. In the end, a frozen pitch produced a game that was far too close for comfort, late second half strikes from Roeder and Goddard eventually sealing the tie 2-0. So instead of a potentially embarrassing replay on the Velcro pitch of Deepdale, we were heading for White Hart Lane in the fifth round and FA Cup favourites, Spurs.

Once again, the temper of the times and the tendency for militant students to demonstrate against the policies of the Thatcher government worked in our favour. A massive National Union of Students rally, protesting against plans for student loans, was organised in Central London to take place on the Saturday of the Spurs game. Lancs. Poly. Students' Union once again thoughtfully provided a subsidised coach trip down to the capital. One bloody quid to get from Preston to London and back! 'Wear Red Please' urged the left-wing propagandists on the back of the coach tickets. We wore black and white!

"You bastards again! How come they're always playing in London when we have something important going on down there?"

"Dunno, ask the FA! Anyway, the FA Cup's more important than your rally."

This time there was a small entourage, as well as the three musketeers, and we took over a section of the bus, singing, no doubt to the annoyance of many at our frivolous intrusion. Still, it passed the time and by now that route, southbound down the M6, was becoming very familiar indeed.

Making the journey from Central London to White Hart Lane entailed a tube ride to Seven Sisters on the Northern Line, followed by a lengthy walk to the ground up Seven Sisters Road. The route was lined by

Standing in the Corner

a frightening cordon of riot police wielding shields, batons and with Alsatians straining at the leash. It was the sort of presence that would be reserved today only for an anti-government rally in the centre of the capital! As we made our way nervously past our minders, it became increasingly apparent that there was almost as much black and white in evidence as indigenous blue and white. Tottenham, underestimating the importance of the early rounds of the cup, had decided not to make the game all-ticket and somewhere in the region of 10,000 Geordies had made the journey south, bolstered by a sizable contingent of Mags exiled in London and the Home Counties. The authorities had recently dealt with what ended up being a three-legged League Cup semi-final derby between Spurs and Arsenal. If they could cope with that then surely they could cope with a few thousand Geordies coming to town for an FA Cup fifth round tie? Wrong!

Not surprisingly, the police and Spurs' security still intended to shoehorn all the travelling supporters into the small corner section of the ground they had reserved. By the time the game was ten minutes old it was getting mightily cramped down at the front near the barrier fence. Some people, mainly kids who couldn't stand the crush, attempted to climb over. Of course, the police tried to force them off the fence and back into the terraces. No one who was at White Hart Lane that day will ever forget it. It was very nearly Hillsborough two years early. Eventually someone must have realised what was going on and the adjacent paddock area, which had been kept empty, was opened to accommodate the overspill. Disaster was averted but it was an early sign of the sort of callous disregard for the safety of football fans that would soon result in one of the worst tragedies in recent British history.

Survival

On the pitch, disaster wasn't averted. The game was settled by a controversial penalty in the first half, converted by the prolific Clive Allen. Albert Craig, a reserve filling in for injury, squandered a golden opportunity to equalise in the final minute and the hosts held out to win 1-0. We were out, but at least we were still alive!

The time-honoured cliché of 'concentrating on the league' was now all too appropriate for Newcastle United. When, the week after Spurs, we lost 1-3 at Division One upstarts Wimbledon, we were left four points adrift at the bottom of the table with 22 points, five points below fourth bottom spot. To make matters worse, the play-offs had been introduced for 1986-87 and the fourth bottom club would have to compete for its First Division life with the teams placed third, fourth and fifth in Division Two. So Newcastle were actually six points behind the last team currently occupying a safe position. There were only fourteen games left. What happened next would even have amazed Houdini!

The following week, Newcastle beat second bottom, and now Hodge-less, Aston Villa 2-1 at St. James' Park. The week after saw Oges, Raj and me run the gauntlet of the Chorlton Street to Maine Road supporters' bus. A 0-0 draw against fellow strugglers City was secured, despite old warhorse Imre Varadi firing over from point-blank range in the dying minutes. Four consecutive home games followed. A tricky midweek clash with Spurs ended 1-1, and three days later we beat lowly Southampton 2-0. The next game, at home to yet another relegation-threatened side, Leicester, was won by two goals in the first five minutes. Finally, on a pleasant April evening in the first week of my Easter break, high-fliers Norwich City were shot down. They'd come to spoil the party, opening the scoring early on, but an equaliser just before the break swung the game. By midway through the second half, we were 4-1 up. Darren Jackson, scorer of the fourth goal, had to be peeled off the fence enclosing the Gallowgate End! Newcastle were on a roll. In the next two games, we drew at Oxford 1-1 and gloriously defeated Arsenal 1-0 at Highbury.

Next came Manchester United and St. James' Park was full to capacity, with thousands locked outside in the car park trying desperately to find a turnstile still open. The momentum continued and Man. U. were slain 2-1, but to many, the most significant event of the day came when Peter Beardsley indicated to the bench that he was injured midway through the second half. A sub was warmed up but when the board went up to signal the replacement, instead of hobbling off, Pedro almost sprinted off the pitch.

It had become increasingly clear that despite the team's improved form, Beardsley was unsettled. There had been an intensive round of tabloid speculation since before Christmas linking our star player to big five clubs, with Liverpool apparently leading the chase. Echoes of the Waddle affair resounded around the North East. At a talk-in I'd attended at a club in Bedlington, Peter stated that he was unhappy with the club's progress and wanted to play in a side that could win trophies and finish in the top six. Fat chance of the penny-pinching board at Newcastle ever financing that!

The next game was a 0-3 defeat at Goodison Park, bringing to an end our nine game unbeaten run. It was no embarrassment, though. Everton were steaming towards a second League Championship in three years and would have beaten anyone on their own ground at that time. A week later we beat Chelsea 2-1 at St. James' and, against all the odds, we were safe - mathematically clear of even the play-offs. The most significant statistic of that run was Paul Goddard

Survival

scoring in eight of the ten games that saw Newcastle avoid relegation. If ever Iam McFaul spent money wisely in his time in the Toon hotseat, it was in bringing Goddard to the club. Of almost equal importance, Paul Gascoigne, who'd missed most of the season through injury, had returned just as the escape plan was being hatched. It had been Gazza's flair and industry that fashioned many of the bullets for Goddard to fire. Another star in the making had signalled his intentions.

The season fizzled out after that. The job was done. The three musketeers only went to one more away game as a unit, the carnival of the final game of the season at Nottingham Forest. Supporters drank, sang and a handful even decided to scale the floodlight pylon sited on the away terrace of the old City Ground!

Raj, however, was determined to take his personal tally of away trips to ten. He'd discovered that another demo in London, with a cheap coach trip, was organised on the Saturday of the second-last away game of the season, West Ham. Oges and I declined, but, undaunted, Raj persuaded a few mates to go with him on the trip. Oh dear! The coach must have been halfway to London before Raj and his pals realised that the 'demonstration' had in fact been organised by the Gay & Lesbian Society! They spent the entire journey back nervously occupying the back seats. Their companions for the journey must have been puzzled at the highly original 'gay chic' in evidence - a striking contrast from the Village People attire that would be on show at most parades! It was a nasty shock for self-styled hardman Raj, a situation he was determined to avoid in future. He brought his own car down the following term!

Seven

Samba at St. James'

In the 1980s, the era of stadium rock, St. James' Park was quick to get in on the act and offer the North East public the increasingly rare chance to see some top names from the world of popular music. These gigs became an annual summer event right the way through to the end of the decade, with such legendary acts as the Rolling Stones and Bruce Springsteen coming to Toon. All most Newcastle United fans wanted to see, though, was a bit of flare on the football pitch, especially as, true to all the tabloid speculation, Peter Beardsley had departed to Liverpool in the summer of 1987 for £1.9 million.

The board of directors had decided to cash in on Pedro a year before the end of his contract, knowing full well that only in those circumstances could the selling club name their price. Two years before, Newcastle had been stung when Chris Waddle's contract had expired before his move to Spurs, leaving the fee to be decided by tribunal. Now, the board were determined not to leave things to chance, and get full valuation for the club's current prize asset. It was a case of financial expedience over long-term planning and it clearly demanded the sale of the England regular in the lucrative summer transfer window a full year before he became a free agent. It would be a highly controversial decision but one which was inevitable, the directors argued, as Peter Beardsley's heart was manifestly no longer at St. James' Park.

Samba at St. James'

Of course, they knew that the fans would be seriously unhappy over the sale of yet another star player, so in a token gesture, a proportion of the sum received for Beardsley was released to Iam McFaul in order to find a replacement. During the previous close season, McFaul's inexperience had led him to waste the whole summer in pursuit of Aberdeen striker John Hewitt, who was actually using Newcastle's interest to stall for time and improve terms for a new contract at Pittodrie. But now, the ex-keeper was a year wiser, and in any case he had a former teammate on the case, making United's cause even stronger. McFaul was determined to get a replacement for Beardsley; even if that meant swallowing up a sizeable part of the large fee the club had received for him, and former Toon favourite Malcolm Macdonald had unearthed an unlikely candidate during the 1987 Rous Cup. That player, in a £625,000 deal brokered by Supermac, was to be Brazilian international striker Mirandinha.

The acquisition of Francisco Ernandi Lima da Silva did exactly what the board had hoped it would. The reaction of the Toon Army to the impending arrival of their new hero was exactly the same in 1987 as the response would be to signings like Shearer, Cole and Ferdinand in the 1990s. The rage at Beardsley's departure was temporarily forgotten and the fans soon had a new song:

We've got Mirandinha, he's not from Argentina,
He's from Brazil, he's f****ing brill!

The ditty was being sung even before Mira played his first game at Norwich City and the little Brazilian did nothing to dampen the hype that already surrounded him. At one point in that game, a 1-1 draw, the Norwich defence lined up a four-man wall as Newcastle's new number 10 stood over a free-kick

Standing in the Corner

awarded on the halfway line! In his second game, Mira scored twice in another score draw, this time with Man. United at Old Trafford. They were both class goals too, the first a diving header and number two a fierce drive from outside the box into the bottom corner of the net. Cue trademark celebrations as Mirandinha wheeled away towards the corner flag, arms outstretched like a plane in take-off! Could it be true? Had Newcastle United signed the biggest sensation to hit English League football in a generation?

Unfortunately, it wasn't. In his next game, at home to Wimbledon, Mira was pushed, shoved and kicked as the Dons effectively marked him out of the game. Wimbledon won 2-1, thereby setting the scene for a season in which they would repeatedly heap disappointment on the Magpies.

Apart from the sight of the Magpies' exciting new striker, the most noticeable feature of St. James' Park in 1987-88 was the ongoing construction work to build a new West Stand. It led to a temporary reduction in ground capacity to just 21,000 but, girder-by-girder, the new structure gradually took shape until it was finally complete just before the end of the season. The main stand's season ticket holders fared a lot worse than their counterparts, inconvenienced by the enlargement of the same part of the ground a decade later. They didn't just lose their roof, the whole stand had been demolished to make way for the new construction and the once proud people of the West Stand were re-housed in a ramshackle seating arrangement sited on the Leazes End.

The promise following the Man. United draw faded still further when Liverpool, parading newly-signed Peter Beardsley, came to town on September 20th. In what was a surprise to many, Beardsley received a warm reception from the terraces and re-paid that compliment by helping his new side batter Newcastle

Samba at St. James'

4-1 in front of the TV cameras. Once again, we reached the end of September sitting at the wrong end of the Division One table, only this time the St. James' Park masses were losing patience, particularly those having to forgo a lot of the comfort to which they were accustomed!

Away from home the faithful remained 100% behind the team at all times, as ever. But after more than a year as a student, my meagre finances were stretched and I knew before the season began I wouldn't be able to afford the away travel I'd managed in the previous campaign. One game that I was able to get to, however, was Coventry in mid-October. The Toon Army was typically upbeat and we had every reason to be. Turning the form book on its head, United swamped the FA Cup holders, winning 3-1 with goals from Darren Jackson, Goddard and Gascoigne. For once, the support from the terraces was repaid on the pitch and the attitude of the players was typified by recent signing John Cornwell, who, in spite of bleeding heavily from a gash to his head, was able to salute the fans as he walked round the pitch for treatment.

For Newcastle, the points total was at last starting to look respectable, while for me impoverishment loomed ever larger in the form of the hard-nosed NatWest bank and a stringent overdraft limit! I was however able to scrape together enough cash for just one more 'away game' soon after the Highfield Road visit, which cost me the princely sum of just 40p.

The major side-effect of the 1986-87 relegation scrap with its underlying injury problems had been felt by Colin Suggett's reserve team, plundered by McFaul to fill the gaps as the first-string clung on to top flight status. The reserves had slipped quietly into the second division of the Central League, starved of their lifeblood as they faced up to the challenge of sides that would have given the NUFC first team a run for its

Standing in the Corner

money. The benefit to me, Oges and any other Newcastle fans marooned in Central Lancashire was that it meant a Newcastle United XI making the journey to Deepdale to play Preston North End in early November.

Deepdale wasn't exactly packed to the rafters for the game - there were more players, coaches and officials than fans on the terraces! Newcastle fielded a team consisting mainly of youngsters for the match and also gave Tommy Wright, recently brought over from Belfast, his first start in the number 1 jersey. But it was a man of far greater experience who stole the show. John Bailey had slipped out of first team contention the previous season and would be released at the end of 87-88, but on that evening he was a revelation, even considering the level of football. Bailey, playing on the left wing, scored a hat-trick and made the other in a keenly contested 4-3 win for the Toon.

About halfway through the first half Raj arrived, late as usual even though he only lived about a quarter of a mile from the ground. We heard him rather than saw him, as he entered the deserted stadium muttering out loud about "North End bashing" (any noun followed by bashing was Raj's favourite footballing term) followed by a small entourage of 'apprentice hooligans' - his student mates from Lancs. Poly. They were all no doubt disappointed to discover no North End fans to bash! Raj was no longer a regular travelling companion of Oges and me, although this had nothing to do with his unfortunate incident at the back end of the previous season! He now had his own car and moved in different student circles. In spite of Raj's absence, and having to miss most away games, Oges and I were still managing to make the journey up to Newcastle every other week. But with home performances often varying from the sublime to the ridiculous, we sometimes wondered why we bothered.

Samba at St. James'

By the end of November, the first team's topsy-turvy form had at least helped us to banish the spectre of another relegation dogfight. One avenue to Wembley had just been closed off by Wimbledon in the League Cup to growing frustration within the Toon Army ranks, but, unbeknown to many of us, our improving league results either side of Christmas were unlocking the gates to another, albeit extremely 'Mickey Mouse', route to the twin towers. By the time Newcastle faced Chelsea at home in late February, it was common knowledge on the St. James' Park terraces that a win would secure a place for us in the Mercantile Football League Centenary Competition at Wembley. Mirandinha's eleventh and twelfth goals of 1987-88, the last in his first season at Newcastle, did the trick, helping us to defeat the relegation-bound Blues 3-1. A place at Wembley guaranteed, then, but first there was some more serious business to attend to. Newcastle had reached the fifth round of the FA Cup again and been handed a home draw, and yet another cup tie against Wimbledon.

United embarked on their second successive cup run on the back of some greatly improved home form. The week before our opening victory over Division Two high-flyers Crystal Palace, we'd deservedly beaten Man. United 1-0 through a goal by Roeder. Similarly, in the match before the fourth round tie with Swindon, Newcastle had turned over Tottenham 2-0. We absolutely murdered Swindon, then, like Palace, quite a useful Second Division team. Cup fever was alive on Tyneside and a big crowd had descended on St. James', now boasting the completed new West Stand. The result was that Oges and I, slightly late for the kick-off, were stuck in a queue for the last remaining turnstile into the Scoreboard as Newcastle raced into an early 2-0 lead. I'd just got in and scampered to the top of the steps when Gascoigne added the third shortly before half-time. Oges didn't appear until the half-time interval.

It was typical of the infrastructure of Newcastle United Football Club in those days - they quite often couldn't organise a piss-up in a brewery, despite the presence of one of the biggest in the country just over the road! There had been no reason for all the turnstiles to be closed in the first place. The crowd was big, but at 29,000 the ground was well short of the recently restored capacity. Gascoigne and emerging forward Michael O'Neill added two further Newcastle goals in the second half and fervent thoughts of Wembley began to form in the minds of the now very expectant Toon Army.

Our home form boded well for the Wimbledon tie. Although they'd beaten us in the league at St. James' early on, and then at Plough Lane in the League Cup, Newcastle were now an attractive side playing neat football centred on the effervescent Gascoigne. This was in stark contrast to Wimbledon's predictable route-one tactics launched from the big boot of Dave Beasant. Newcastle would murder Wimbledon if we could get Gazza going and the Dons knew it. The game at St. James' Park was billed as the tie of the round and the Football League computer had considerably arranged for a dress rehearsal to be played at Plough Lane the week before.

Wimbledon's tactics may have been rudimentary but the self-styled Crazy Gang's understanding of how to intimidate opponents was honed to a fine art. They used the league match to put this into practice. The Dons possessed a young midfielder whose thuggish approach to the game had earned him the nickname Psycho. In an incident that has since gone down in folklore, Vinnie Jones repeatedly made a point of providing Gascoigne with a painful below the belt greeting every time their paths crossed. The Plough

Samba at St. James'

Lane club might not have expected that one of Jones' ball-breakers would appear, the following morning, on the back page of nearly all the Sunday newspapers. But the effect it would have on Gazza's confidence in the impending cup tie was everything they could've dreamed of!

If Wimbledon were the underdogs, they certainly weren't showing any fear of Newcastle as the big match got underway. Gascoigne, by contrast, was anything but his usual cocky and brilliant self. Wimbledon managed to dominate the opening passages of play, as the Magpies' midfield was unable to get the ball down and hold onto it. Gazza just seemed to want to avoid Jones at all times, allowing the Dons' assassin the freedom of midfield whenever the ball was on the ground anywhere near the centre circle. The away team's dominance had to tell eventually and before the interval Wimbledon scored, giving them a one-goal advantage at the break.

Half-time was misery where I was standing, in the West Stand paddock right beside the Leazes End away supporters' enclosure. There were only about two dozen of them and, unlike almost any other away fans I'd ever seen, they didn't even seem bothered that their team was 1-0 up away from home in the FA Cup fifth round. It would almost have been merciful if they'd bothered to goad us, like most other teams would. Instead, there was this niggling feeling of injustice that the proud Toon Army, 29,000 strong, had to surrender to a glorified Southern League club with no fans and talentless big-boot footballers. I let my feelings get the better of me and bellowed as much towards the twenty-four Wimbledon supporters. Not surprisingly, the Dons continued to show cool disinterest in the events going on around them and all I gained from my outburst was a frosty glare from a police officer standing nearby! In the second half, The Crazy Gang continued where they'd left off, adding to their lead and eventually winning the tie 3-1. The last great hope of almost all Newcastle supporters in 1987-88 was dashed. But was the Wembley dream really dead?

Well, if I wasn't going to get to Wembley in the FA Cup, now I certainly wasn't going to miss the opportunity in the Mickey Mouse Mercantile Centenary competition! The problem was a complete lack of interest from any of my mates. The principal three at the time, Oges, Raj and Paul from Ashington, unlike me, had all been before, to the 1976 League Cup Final as kids. None felt the urge to travel down to London for such an inauspicious occasion. Indeed, most Newcastle supporters felt likewise, even if they hadn't been to Wembley before. They would only go to watch Newcastle play in a proper competition - the Full Member's Cup even - but not this. Predictably, ticket sales didn't take-off, especially as the draw now pitted us against Liverpool in the first round and, in the unlikely event of progress, probably Wimbledon in the second. Undaunted, during my Easter break I made my way to the old Supporters' Club shop round the corner from Haymarket and bought myself a ticket. Back down in Preston, my bank manager took out a calculator, did some arithmetic and frowned. What the f***! I was going down there to see the Toon play come hell or high water.

The road to Wembley the following weekend was a far from smooth one. First it involved an overnight journey south by coach, travelling by myself and during which I couldn't get a wink of sleep. Then I was left with an hour and a half to kill before the tubes started as the bus had arrived at Victoria coach station at 6am. The earliest I could get to Wembley was eight, still two hours before the competition kicked off, but at least it was an infinitely more pleasant environment than Victoria. This was my first visit to the Twin

Samba at St. James'

Towers and for the uninitiated like myself, even at a minor event like this, the thousands of supporters milling around outside the stadium and the stalls ringing the ground selling merchandise added up to an enthralling sight. The environment once I got inside left me a little disappointed. Far from being a glistening shrine to the English game, ramshackle Wembley Stadium was a crumbling reminder of past glories far removed from the place I'd imagined it to be.

Once events got under way, the Toon Army didn't have too long to wait for Newcastle's opening match. The format for the first day of the competition, on Saturday 16th April 1988, was straight knockout, with games being of two halves of 20 minutes duration and sudden-death penalties to decide a drawn tie. The Toon were up second, following the surprise defeat of Cup Finalists Wimbledon by fourth division Tranmere. It would take a result almost as shocking as that just seen for Newcastle to progress. Liverpool, the other Cup Finalists, were at the last count approximately 100 points clear at the top of Division One - they'd only lost one game all season, against Everton in the League Cup. The way most of us saw it, the pubs in Wembley Centre would just be opening after we got knocked out.

We were not, in the end, destined to be at the bar by 11.30. The game ended 0-0; Liverpool, like Wimbledon before them, were really only going through the motions. So it was penalties! Neil McDonald converted the first spot-kick for Newcastle and now Liverpool had to score. Amazingly, little Gary Kelly, who'd taken over from Martin Thomas in goal, saved from Aldridge and we were through to a Quarter-Final meeting with Tranmere. The two thousand or so Toon Army stalwarts celebrated an unlikely victory as Liverpool strode from the pitch none-too-bothered by the result.

The glory was short-lived. Tranmere were fired up for the second round match taking place at 1 o'clock,

Standing in the Corner

whilst Newcastle's players, Gazza included, seemed to believe they just had to turn up and the Merseyside minnows would collapse. In situations like that there's usually only one outcome - the minnows prevail - and they did 2-0, with McDonald ingloriously missing a second-half penalty that would have made the scores level. Once again pride had come before a fall for Newcastle United.

Worse was to follow for me because one of my best mates back home in Morpeth, a lad called Stokesey, was a dyed-in-the-wool Tranmere fan. I managed to negotiate my way out of Wembley without seeing him, departing at the same time as me in the middle of a scrum of ecstatic Tranmere supporters. I was even able not to run into him on any of my periodic visits back home for a further three months, steering clear of any of his known haunts to avoid abuse for our Wembley debacle. This period of grace could never last. It was a summer evening in Morpeth and my guard was down as I walked across the narrow footbridge crossing the River Wansbeck between Bridge Street and Castle Square. In the opposite direction came Stokesey. Shit! What should I do? I decided not to turn round and run in the opposite direction, dignity was the better option! Especially as I was in a party that included a couple of girls - I couldn't show fear; I'd just have to face the music. The Scouser was as scathing as I expected, but at least it was done. I could get on with my life as a football supporter knowing that the humiliation was over!

The only problem was, for Newcastle fans the real humiliation was just about to begin. For the rest of that season however, the Magpies' results were highly encouraging. A 4-0 win over Luton at St. James' Park was the highlight, a game in which the rapidly developing Michael O'Neill scored a hat-trick. The Newcastle players exacted revenge on their Luton

Samba at St. James'

counterparts for the Hatters' unsporting antics during a reverse of that scoreline earlier in the season at Kenilworth Road. Shortly after the fourth goal went in, Newcastle started passing the ball round aimlessly among themselves, giving it back to Kelly every time a Luton player encroached. The Luton players - a miserable bunch, accurately reflecting their miserable football club - complained to the referee, who rightly did nothing. Every now and again, someone would start a session of keepie-up just to goad Luton even more and eventually, to the delight of the fans, Kenny Wharton sat down on the ball for a few seconds to prolong their agony still further! It was a memorable moment that sealed local lad Kenny a place in the hearts of the Toon Army as he entered his testimonial season. After the game I celebrated by getting totally wasted at The Sun Inn in Morpeth. I'd bumped into a lad called Michael Bolam on the way home, an old mate from school, who nowadays is an authority on the Toon and helps run the NUFC.com website. One pint turned into eight. Drinking Brown Ale on an empty stomach is never a good idea but in those days Newcastle didn't win 4-0 every week!

Newcastle won four of their last six Division One matches to finish eighth in the table, relegating Watford and Portsmouth in the final week of the campaign. Nonetheless, the season finished on an ominous note - John Robertson, a prolific centre forward north of the border, was signed from Hearts well after the transfer deadline. The more knowledgeable men of St. James' knew exactly what this meant - someone was leaving, probably the highly popular Paul Goddard, who hadn't exactly hit it off with his new Brazilian strike partner Mirandinha. Goddard did indeed leave, moving to Derby County to be closer to his family, who were now living back down in London. He would be sorely missed. Even more

Standing in the Corner

ominously, the by-now familiar round of tabloid press speculation had been growing ever louder as the season died linking Paul Gascoigne with a multi-million pound transfer to Spurs. Newcastle United, it seemed, were about to sell yet another star player.

Eight

Sack The Board

During the summer of 1988, as speculation over Gazza's future on Tyneside turned into a £2.6 million deal taking him to White Hart Lane, a consortium sensing the despair of the Toon Army launched an aggressive takeover bid for control of Newcastle United. The Magpie Group, fronted by Cameron-Hall plc chairman John Hall and consisting of high profile North East business and industry figures, was an impressive organisation. Oozing business acumen, the would-be new owners produced a slick portfolio promising to inject large sums of cash to redevelop the ground, fund team-building and launch a share issue to raise additional funds and democratise the club. The key phrase in all the proposals was 'speculate to accumulate' - the principle that all the big five clubs followed to sustain their relentless pursuit of silverware. The Magpie Group maintained that if the Geordie public were given a team to be proud of and a stadium worthy of the name, then crowds of over 40,000 would flock to St. James' Park on a weekly basis. That, they explained, would make team-building on a 'Big Five' scale self-financing.

The incumbent board of directors was by contrast an amalgam of butcher, baker and candlestick-maker type characters, whose families had held the controlling interest in Newcastle United for generations, since they were the business elite of Tyneside. Now though, they had had no cash, no ambition and had only rebuilt part of the ground because they were given no alternative. Their blueprint for the future of Newcastle United was crystal clear. Sell off the best players to achieve a profit in the transfer market, use the cash from the healthy attendance figures to pay off the cost of the West Stand reconstruction and, above-all, cling on for dear life to First Division status, the only thing that guaranteed those gates remaining as they were. Trophies and top-six finishes were a luxury Newcastle United could no longer afford.

When Big Five clubs needed to raise money in times of emergency or for team strengthening, they would quite often bring new blood into the boardroom, thereby raising the much needed cash. The Newcastle board's response to initial feelers put out by Magpie Group members was to close ranks, knowing that the antiquated constitution of the club could work in their favour in the event of a hostile bid. They had taken this line before, some six years earlier, when millionaire AC/DC lead singer Brian Johnston, a lifelong Mag, had offered to inject cash into the club in return for a place on the board.

Needless to say, the long-suffering fans were 110% behind the Magpie Group. John Hall's name had been chanted at St. James' Park games towards the end of the previous season, but a takeover involving a modern plc was one thing. Newcastle United's constitution wasn't the only thing that was antiquated, the shareholding, originally floated in the late nineteenth century, was scattered all over the former British Empire, many shares long forgotten about and effectively lost. Under the voting system, any party seeking to take a controlling interest in the limited company needed first to get 70% to force a confidence vote against the standing directors. This would be impossible to achieve without the acquisition of a portion of shares already in the hands of current board members. The chairman, Gordon McKeag, had recently likened his family's interest in Newcastle United to "the family silver" and the board had long referred to the fans as "customers". Given this resolve to maintain the status quo, any successful takeover was going to be long, hard and extremely expensive. Fortunately for the Toon Army, John Hall had patience, strength and, crucially, wads of cash!

The situation Newcastle United now found itself in was entirely down to the board's desire to keep the club 'in the family'. The loyalty of the fans and the help of the now dispensed with sponsorship of Scottish & Newcastle Breweries had enabled them to run the club on a shoestring for years without experiencing the crippling financial difficulties suffered by clubs like Wolves and Middlesbrough. The fans had, Jack Charlton's tactics apart, been very understanding in the first three seasons back in the top flight, during which time the club had gone absolutely nowhere near to winning anything and sold off for huge profit the best three players it had produced in a generation.

Frustration had been building long before 1988, but it was the FA Cup exit at the hands of Wimbledon that brought matters to a head. It didn't help that little Wimbledon, a non-league club the last time Newcastle had played in a Wembley cup final, went on and lifted the trophy, but it still wouldn't have mattered if they hadn't. Wimbledon's success was only the straw that broke the camel's back in the minds of the fans. In the previous three seasons Norwich, Oxford, Coventry and Luton had all won major domestic cup competitions - they were all smaller clubs than Newcastle. West Ham had mounted a credible title challenge. Even Sunderland had played in a major cup final in recent seasons. Newcastle's total lack of ambition was scandalous and the world-class players we'd produced had voted with their feet! Now the Toon Army wanted to be up there challenging for honours with the big five on a regular basis, and that required some new blood with the impetus and drive to realise those ambitions. There was only one thing for it: the old board of directors would have to go!

Nine

McFaul-Guy

The problem with selling clubs is that sooner or later they sell a player they then find impossible to replace. If Newcastle had got away with the sale of Waddle because of the emergence of a world-class Peter Beardsley, and likewise the sale of Beardsley through the fulfilment of Paul Gascoigne's potential, they were about to find out that Gazza was in fact that one irreplaceable jewel in the crown. The board had again sanctioned big money spending in the summer to redress the sales of Gascoigne, Goddard and Neil McDonald. Wimbledon's cup-final penalty stopper Dave Beasant and centre half Andy Thorn, plus pacy forward John Hendrie from Bradford, all joined John Robertson on the Gallowgate books.

There was, however, to be no replacement brought in to fill the crucial central midfield role vacated by Gazza's exit. Instead, the responsibility fell on the shoulders of Ian Bogie, another of the crop of young hopefuls from the Youth Cup winners of three years before. Bogie had been unable to make an impression on the first team picture owing to the presence of Gascoigne; still, the board (who labelled him the new Gazza) and, to a less hysterical extent, McFaul extolled the virtues of their untried midfield general. It was a terrible burden to place on the shoulders of a young and still highly inexperienced player.

In a pre-season friendly at Portland Park, Bogie found it hard to dominate the action in centre midfield against Northern League Division Two outfit Ashington. He would find it infinitely harder still against Football League Division One opposition. Although the unfortunate Bogie proved to be a more than useful player for Preston North End and Port Vale in the reformed League Divisions One and Two, to expect him to pitch straight into a relegation dogfight with next to no first team experience was asking too much. McFaul would pay a heavy price as Newcastle made their worst start to a League campaign since 1978.

The new season started ominously enough. Newcastle found themselves a goal down inside 60 seconds at Goodison Park with Everton running out 4-0 winners against the clueless Magpies. They too had extensively rebuilt their side, having just signed the scorer of that first minute goal, Tony Cottee, and taken Neil McDonald south from Tyneside, though unlike McFaul, Colin Harvey seemed to have achieved some balance to his squad.

The following weekend threw up a peach of a fixture as the St. James' Park curtain raiser - Tottenham with Waddle and Gascoigne making an early return visit. 33,508 crammed into the ground for the big showdown, all eager to welcome back Gateshead's two most famous sons. Gazza didn't know what sort of reception to expect - the rough ride experienced by his new teammate in 85-86 or the warm applause enjoyed by Beardsley sixteen months later. He didn't have to wait long to find out. As he jogged out for the warm-up, raising his arms to applaud the crowd a resonant "BOOOO...!" echoed from every corner of St. James' Park. Sauntering cautiously towards the Gallowgate End to join his colleagues for a knockabout, a shower of Mars bars rained down at him from the terraces in such number it was soon impossible to see the grass in the six-yard area. Gazza walked over and picked one up and pretended to eat it, but this failed to pacify the fans - he was just pelted with more! Spurs' new number 8 beat a hasty retreat.

The game opened with Newcastle throwing everything at Spurs. Maybe those signings weren't so bad after all... we were playing brilliantly. United took the lead midway through the first half and soon after went 2-0 up. As Darren Jackson celebrated the second goal, the most amazing sight appeared above the Gallowgate End. There, in immaculate liquid crystal detail, Jackson's mugshot beamed down from the scoreboard. A brand new state-of-the-art board had been installed in the close season by NEI, Tyneside's leading high-tech electrical manufacturer. Not since 1985, when the previous board's little jumping men that celebrated a goal last performed, had we possessed a fully functional scoreboard. Oh what joy!

It was carnival time in the Gallowgate and the fans now turned on Gascoigne with a vengeance. "Fat-boy what's the score? Fat-boy, Fat-boy what's the score?" demanded supporters that a few months earlier had been singing his praises. It was more than the lad from just over the river at Dunston could take; he was shrinking ever further into his shell. As he would two years later in the World Cup semi-final, he shambled around the pitch almost in tears, trying to stay as close to Waddle as possible.

The Waddler, of course, knew how to deal with these situations but even he wasn't prepared for what happened next. Terry Venables replaced the delirious Gascoigne at half-time and Spurs came out a new side. Newcastle were cocky and, just like three seasons before, got caught out with Waddle nicking a goal back straight from the re-start. By the time rejuvenated Spurs had levelled the scores, things were getting a bit ugly and the crowd switched focus onto Waddle. As he went over to take a corner at the Gallowgate End, a

Standing in the Corner

hail of leftover Mars bars were hurled at him. Soft-centred confectionary is one thing - it tends not to comprise a lethal projectile when thrown from the terraces - but a lump of concrete is another matter! Some dickhead had managed to prise a piece of the terracing off and decided to throw it at the England winger as he lined up the set-piece, missing by only a few yards. Not surprisingly, Waddle was for once visibly shaken by this mindless act. The game became something of a non-event thereafter and fizzled out into a 2-2 stalemate. It was more a case of two points dropped than one gained and, as a consequence of the actions of one brain-dead moron, the club closed the entire corner section of the Gallowgate voluntarily for the next home game. It may have seemed an extreme measure to take but it almost certainly avoided more draconian sanctions being imposed by the FA.

Following a meaningless and extremely dull extra-time win over Wimbledon in the Centenary Cup competition, we were off the following Saturday to Derby County in the league. I found myself in Preston two weeks early to clear up some outstanding coursework from my previous year's study, meaning I could hitch a lift to the game with Oges. So too was another Lancs. Poly Mag - Andy, a lad from Ashington, who'd drifted into travelling to Newcastle games with us the previous season. He was now becoming something of a full-time fan and, in any case, made a far better travelling companion than Raj.

Arthur Cox had done an even more impressive job at Derby than he had at Newcastle. He'd inherited a team recently relegated to Division Three in 1984, and in just three seasons had led them back up into the top flight. Cox had just added Paul Goddard to his squad in the close season, of course, and Derby's impressive blend of youth and experience were the outside bet of many for a top-six finish that year. They certainly looked a better side than us as Newcastle were repeatedly opened up in the first half. The only thing Derby couldn't do was finish. John Anderson was having a torrid time at left-back as he tried to deal with the energetic Derby wideman Gary Micklewhite. Oges, in those days, had a tendency to dwell unfavourably on the performances of a select few Newcastle players who he didn't feel were up to the job. Following the departure of Neil McDonald, the current incumbent as his bête-noir was Anderson. He was, according to Oges, "playing like he'd had a drink before the game". Finally, satisfied that his assertion was correct, Oges decided to confront the Newcastle number 3 as he was skinned once more by Micklewhite just in front of where we were standing.

"Oi, Anderson! You're not supposed to drink before you play football," he bellowed, adding, "and you're bloody useless even when you're sober!"

The Irishman jogged back after his latest failure to prevent the passage of his opposite number, apparently unmoved by this comparison to his international teammate Paul McGrath!

As the game moved into the last quarter of an hour, it was still goalless with Derby having pressed for almost the whole 75 minutes. We were just beginning to believe that we might hold out for a share of the points when Micklewhite for once cut inside Anderson and curled a left foot shot past the helpless Beasant from thirty yards. A minute later it was two and all hope was dead. The following week the crisis deepened with another 0-2 defeat, this time at home to Norwich. By the time I got back to Preston in late September, Newcastle were in that all-too familiar position at the bottom of the pile with just two points from five games. We had also just lost embarrassingly 0-3 at Third Division Sheffield United in the League Cup. Ominous signs of a gloomy relegation scrap were already beginning to appear.

Standing in the Corner

In the Eighties there was never a good time to go to Anfield and play Liverpool, but given Newcastle's circumstances, such a visit surely couldn't have come at a worse time. As Andy, Oges and I jostled for position in the packed Anfield Road End, we were uneasy in the memory that the previous season Newcastle had let in four goals home and away against the Reds. What humiliation was about to befall us with our new squad of no-hopers? All our worst fears began to materialise when Gary Gillespie headed in from a Liverpool corner inside the first ten minutes. Somehow Liverpool subsequently just seemed to blow chance after chance while we remained in mortal fear of them adding to their lead. Then, with only minutes to go to half-time, we got a lifeline. John Hendrie used his pace to scamper away from the Liverpool defence and fire an unlikely equaliser across Mike Hooper against the run of play.

The Anfield Road End was suddenly in high spirits as at last the Toon Army had something to celebrate. As the game wore on, we even began to believe we might hold out for a draw. Then, in the 80th minute, the most incredible thing happened - the referee, Mr. Peck, awarded Newcastle a penalty in front of the Kop. It must be a dream, surely - referees just didn't give penalties against Liverpool at Anfield! The suspense was unbearable as Mirandinha stepped up to take it. I was sure he was going to sky it, but the Brazilian kept his cool, sending Hooper the wrong way and the Toon Army into fevered celebration. If the suspense of Mirandinha's run-up had been unbearable then that of the last ten minutes play was worse! Liverpool always looked dangerous and you thought that they only had to get the ball into our box and they would equalise. Thank God - they didn't. It was easily the most important victory of my, Oges or Andy's time as Newcastle supporters and we were determined to milk it when we got back to Preston.

The first to suffer was fellow student Neil, a glory-hunting Liverpool supporter from Coventry who was a season ticket-holder on the Kop. He'd affected an irritating pseudo-Scouse accent, even though he hadn't even the vaguest Merseyside connections. Oges and I had waited a whole two years for an opportunity to gloat at this bastard's expense and the experience was well worth the wait! Then it was off into town in full colours to celebrate with several pints of Lancashire's finest ale. You might think such behaviour, given the times, was highly provocative deep in enemy territory. Not a bit! Apart from a handful of "success-supporters", Central Lancashire was a bastion of Scouse-hatred in those days. The main NatWest bank in Preston had recently been the victim of an armed robbery by a Liverpudlian gang and on the local late night radio phone-in, the equivalent of Metro's *Night Owls*, presenter Alan Beswick used to regularly ban all Scousers from the show to popular acclaim from the Lancashire-based listeners! We received warm congratulations from Preston supporters in all the bars we went in. It just so happened that North End had won at home and many of our acquaintances were also out enjoying an extended post-match celebration. Winning at Anfield, back then, was like winning the cup and at long last we were able to bask in a little glory courtesy of our team. The sweet taste of success was to be extremely short-lived!

In the following week we were brought back to reality with a resounding thump. Newcastle United, capable of beating Champions Liverpool at Anfield, were unable to claw back the deficit in the second leg against lowly Sheffield United. Then, on the following Saturday, we found ourselves 0-3 down at half-time against Coventry at St. James' Park. It was more than many of the long-suffering fans in the West Stand could take and members of the board were abused and jostled as they attempted to reach the safety of the

Standing in the Corner

boardroom during the interval. That in turn was more than they could take and they took their anger out on the manager in the wake of another humiliating defeat.

Iam McFaul's tenure as Newcastle boss was ended the day after the passing was announced of the club's most revered servant, Jackie Milburn. Such disrespectful timing could have been understood if the board had a replacement lined up to take over. No chance! What followed was an embarrassing series of rejections as the manager's job at Newcastle was given the cold shoulder in much the same way as the England coach's position after the resignation of Graham Taylor. And why shouldn't the cream of British coaching talent regard it with such dread? After all, you would be expected to sell-on any world-class talent that emerged to your strongest opponents and any money that was available would be less than that brought in by sales. Of the previous three incumbents, two had resigned - one over a lack of transfer money - and the other had been sacked after being forced to sell two world-class players in the preceding fourteen months. Then there was the added uncertainty that a successful Magpie Group takeover could spell an early bath for any new coach they didn't fancy!

Reserve team coach Colin Suggett was put in temporary charge of first team affairs while the list of rejections grew longer. Even the Man from Del Monte would probably have said "No" to Newcastle!

Fans' favourites Howard Kendall and, not surprisingly, Arthur Cox quickly ruled themselves out. There were strong indications that the board had got their man when a press conference was apparently called to announce the appointment of former Celtic boss David Hay. If there was any truth in that rumour then Hay jilted Newcastle at the altar, as the press conference never went ahead. As the uncertainty continued, the board decided to assume executive responsibility in the transfer market. The result was one of the most notorious transfer failures in the history of the club. One Rob MacDonald, an English journeyman player of lower division quality, was on trial at Newcastle whilst in employment in Dutch league football. A board member apparently saw MacDonald, a centre forward, score a goal on the training ground at Benwell and immediately recommended that he be signed, forthwith. The rest of the directors agreed, presumably believing such a name, when teamed-up with the number 9 shirt, must have magical healing properties for an ailing Newcastle United team!

With Christmas fast approaching, it seemed Newcastle would not find a replacement for McFaul easily. Results, if anything, got worse under Suggett and, as the teams occupying the safe positions got further away, United remained rooted to the foot of the Division One table.

Ten

The Eagle Has Landed

Newcastle had long possessed a reputation for managerial appointments as unambitious as their activity in the transfer market. Even success stories like Joe Harvey and Arthur Cox lacked reputations, pre-United, outside lower division coaching. Only Jack Charlton, with Middlesbrough and Sheffield Wednesday on his CV, could be regarded as anywhere near high profile. So when eventually the club announced that they'd appointed a new manager, it came as something of a surprise to discover he was someone we'd actually heard of!

Jim Smith, known throughout the game as 'The Bald Eagle', had progressed smoothly through non-league and lower division management and earned his considerable reputation by steering Oxford United through successive promotions from the Third Division to the First. After falling out with Oxford's dodgy chairman Robert Maxwell, Smith then moved to QPR, leading them to the League Cup final in 1987 and a top-six finish in Division One the following year. There was no doubting his track record, but all of Smith's success had come with improving the lot of smaller clubs. Was he now capable of the transition to a big, under-achieving and desperately struggling football club?

The Bald Eagle wasn't prepared to make do with what he'd inherited. He publicly stated that the squad was relegation fodder and immediately set about

The Eagle Has Landed

making wholesale changes to a side that was but three players short of the one that finished eighth the previous May. Smith went for experience, bringing in full-backs Ray Ranson and Kenny Sansom, Man. United's utility player Liam O'Brien and the midfielder widely blamed for Everton's 'Road to Damascus' revival four years earlier, Kevin Brock. Two Danish internationals followed, midfielder Benny Kristensen and another ineffective forward, Frank Pingel. Immediately out of the door went Dave Beasant to Chelsea, seen as too much of a luxury player for a relegation battle. He was followed by many of McFaul's younger first team players: Darren Jackson and Michael O'Neill both left to pursue successful careers north of the border, left-back Brian Tinnion went to become one of Bristol City's best loved players and Paul Stephenson headed south for Millwall muttering something about improving his England prospects. He still didn't get capped! Finally John Robertson, who'd never fitted in, was sold back to Hearts for the same fee Newcastle had paid for him in April.

Following a 3-0 win at home over newly-promoted Middlesbrough, Newcastle then went six consecutive league games without scoring a goal. There were close but disappointing 0-1 defeats to title contenders Forest and Arsenal at St. James' Park. Then there were embarrassingly one-sided away defeats to QPR and Millwall, 0-3 and 0-4 respectively. Smith's arrival in late November temporarily arrested the slide.

Back-to-back 0-0 draws with Man. United and Luton were enhanced by only the second home win of the season over Wimbledon. Then another draw at St. James' followed, a 3-3 thriller versus fellow strugglers Southampton, a game which saw Rob MacDonald put in his only decent performance for the Magpies, starring in the second-half comeback from 1-3 down. On Boxing Day we beat Sheffield Wednesday at

Hillsborough, but the wheels would well and truly come off the revival before the decorations were off the Christmas tree! On New Year's Eve United went down 0-2 at Spurs, beginning another winless sequence that would last into February.

Newcastle played more games in the 1989 FA Cup campaign than in either of the previous two seasons, when we'd progressed to the fifth round. The only problem was that all four matches comprised the same third round tie against Watford. By the time the Hornets had won the third replay 1-0 thanks to a Roeder own goal, we'd played seven and a half hours of cup football in eleven days. Not ideal preparation for a crucial relegation six-pointer.

Oges' car was packed for the journey south to Aston Villa on second weekend in January. Not only was there the driver, Andy and me, as usual - Oges' girlfriend Lesley was going shopping in Birmingham and there was also a student friend of ours, Hewel, going to the match as well. Hewel, a Welshman, was no Newcastle fan but had periodically travelled to games with us before, just for something to do. More importantly, Taff-Man as he was known, possessed unique powers - in the ten or so matches he'd been to, Newcastle had never lost. He hadn't been to any games with us so far this season and now, for such an important fixture, we felt it necessary to persuade him to accompany us once again!

Taff-Man's magic seemed to be working when Newcastle were awarded a penalty converted by Mirandinha to give us a 1-0 lead. We hadn't really looked like scoring! With Villa desperately attacking the away end in search of an equaliser and only half an hour left, we now needed to defend resolutely and hold out for the three points. In games like this, when things are going your way, it usually takes a mistake of catastrophic proportions to turn the tide. Liam

The Eagle Has Landed

O'Brien, deputising as centre-half made the blunder. Under no real pressure and trying to play out time, O'Brien committed the cardinal sin of playing the ball square across the face of the area towards his central defensive partner, Kevin Scott. The pass never made it - Villa's alert centre-forward Alan McInally read O'Brien's intention, intercepted and fired past Gary Kelly to equalise. It was all downhill after that. Villa, revitalised, scored twice more and strolled to a 3-1 win. Taff-Man's luck had run out!

A brace of home games offered some hope after Villa, but the following week we surrendered tamely to an unimpressive Charlton Athletic. Afterwards, the sickened Toon Army staged a "Sack the Board" protest, a non-violent demonstration outside the ground, nonetheless broken up by mounted police wielding batons. The protests were gathering momentum, thanks in no small part to the rise of Newcastle United's first and now only fanzine *The Mag*. Compared to today's slick magazine, *The Mag* was more like a comic in its infancy, but nevertheless it was the first properly written publication to focus the growing tide of opinion against the board. At times, it sailed extremely close to the wind with some of the rhetoric it aimed at the directors, often making comical references to such subjects as Gordon McKeag's sporting prowess and physical state. The humorous light in which it dealt with such serious matters was at least a welcome source of amusement in those dismal times. And the hilarious comic strips like Dick Dastard (He's a Mackem B****) and Walker Dan certainly helped prevent many fans from climbing to the top of the Tyne Bridge after several of United's inept performances that season!

Ironically, Newcastle were outstanding in the next match, against mighty Liverpool, taking an early lead through Mirandinha and almost snatching all three points when Hendrie narrowly missed making it 3-2 in the 90th minute. It almost turned into another mini-revival with a 2-1 away win over Coventry the week after and then a 1-1 draw at Ayresome Park with Middlesbrough, a Sunday game for which Oges had managed to get us tickets in the Holgate End! Not knowing one end of Chemical Alley from the other, we walked in, in full colours, just as O'Brien opened the scoring for Newcastle! Unsurprisingly, the home supporters were aggrieved at our intrusion, however innocent, and we were hastily offered a police escort round the pitch to the away enclosure under a hail of coins thrown by the Orcs.

The next Saturday though, grimly, things were back to normal. We lost at home again, this time 1-2 to QPR; Newcastle hadn't started to play until we were 2-0 down. Raj, who'd made a rare trip with Oges and me, completely missed Ranson's late consolation goal as he was staging a solo sit-down protest with his back to the pitch. Fortunately we were on the smaller Leazes End terrace that day - on the Gallowgate, Raj would've probably been trampled to death in the crowd surge!

Briefly, hope again sprang from despair. In the next three games Newcastle drew away with Forest and beat Everton and Norwich consecutively, 2-0. Was the mouse about to get out of the trap like in '87? Not likely! Following the Easter Saturday victory at Carrow Road, on Easter Monday we crashed 1-3 at St. James' in a crucial six-point face-off with Sheffield Wednesday. We didn't win another game all season.

Newcastle United didn't get much right in that dismal campaign. In the next game at St. James', another six-pointer lost to Villa, the new scoreboard boldly announced Little Polvier, winner of the 1989 Grand National, as Liverpool Bear! The champion racehorse was in fact named after a renowned salmon pool on the Royal Aberdeenshire Dee, but unlike

The Eagle Has Landed

Merseyside's high flyers, the once noble Newcastle United now seemed a far from distinguished sporting phenomenon. A disgruntled season ticket-holder in what was now respectfully re-named the Milburn Stand, displaced to a scaffold in 1987-88 and forced to watch the NUFC equivalent of the Death March in 88-89, attempted to sue the club for the price of his ticket under the Trade Descriptions Act. He reckoned that entertainment was an unfair and inaccurate description of the merchandise for which he had paid! United were only spared the embarrassment of a court case because football clubs were exempt from the legislation. It all added further weight to the Magpie Group's cause and by the end of the season they'd already bought-out two former directors. Their forward momentum was the only vague suggestion of a silver lining to the black relegation cloud hanging over Gallowgate by May.

The curtain came down on Newcastle's five-year spell in the top flight at Old Trafford, the Magpies losing 0-2 and finishing bottom, nine points adrift of safety. The Newcastle supporters sang, "We'll meet again" to the well spread-out 30,000 Reds inside the ground in what was a cordial atmosphere between the two sets of fans. How things would change!

As the Hillsborough Disaster cast an even darker cloud over the entire game of football, it was a time to be philosophical about something like relegation. Still, the faithful Toon Army felt badly let down and had every right to do so. A crowd average of 22,907 - another statistic of note - was maintained despite the miserable performances and after the abject failure of their regime, the board was still refusing to relinquish control. If they'd had such a thing as a five-year plan it clearly hadn't worked; why didn't they just walk away and let someone else who might just make a success of the venture have a go? Whatever happened, for the next year at least, we would have to get used to the absence of top-level football at St. James' Park and endure visits to places like Oakwell, Dean Court and Home Park. It was back to the hard times for the Toon Army.

Eleven

Promotion or Bust

The emphasis for Newcastle United Football Club was now to bounce straight back into Division One at the first attempt. Jim Smith once again rang the changes for what would be the sort of campaign he had made his name in. The steadfast Roeder and McCreery were allowed to depart, both nearing the end of their careers anyway; they'd given sterling service to the club. Kenny Sansom, who'd looked like his career ended before he left Arsenal, moved to QPR and Mirandinha, seen as unlikely to be of use in Division Two, went back to his old club Palmeiras in Brazil on loan. The ineffective strikers MacDonald and Pingel both made for the exit too.

In the other direction, a host of new faces and one that was vaguely familiar walked into St. James' Park during the summer months of 1989. The vaguely familiar face was that of Mark McGhee, who'd briefly played for Newcastle under Bill McGarry in the late 70s before making his name north of the border with Aberdeen and Celtic. Smith had resolved to pair the clever Scottish attacker with the more direct but nonetheless prolific Mick Quinn, a somewhat rotund Scouser with a liking for pies and racehorses. Other major signings included firebrand midfielder Kevin Dillon, winger Wayne Fereday, veteran goalkeeper John 'Budgie' Burridge, along with youngsters Mark Stimson, Darren Bradshaw and the exciting Scot, John Gallacher.

Standing in the Corner

Newcastle's rivals for promotion were numerous. Apart from the other relegated clubs, Middlesbrough and West Ham, there were several more big clubs in the Division. Leeds, Wolves and Sunderland had all been out of the top flight for several years and were eager to get back, with Leeds in particular now punching with the financial might of a would-be First Division club. It was Newcastle though, with gates expected to be much greater than all of their rivals, that was seen as the biggest fish in the Second Division pond. There was some doubt within the club, however, as to whether those gates would remain as high as they'd been in previous seasons. Relegation had had a profound effect on crowds at St. James' Park in 1978 and concerns were high, especially as a group calling itself 'United Supporters For Change' had irresponsibly called for a boycott of home matches. The Magpie Group, the focus of any likely changes at the club, dismissed such talk and urged fans to keep going. Their appeals were heard and 24,396 were at St. James' Park for the opening game of the season against Leeds.

Somehow St. James' Park felt different after five years in Division One, but a firecracker of a game soon put away any thoughts of inferiority. It was a chance for all the new faces to show their worth to the Toon Army and they didn't disappoint. Young Gallacher was particularly impressive. Quinny's first contribution was to produce an air shot as a ball flashed across the face of the six-yard box. Moments later he'd scored his first goal for Newcastle, firing home a penalty at the Gallowgate End. 1-0! Although Leeds hit back twice to lead 2-1 at the break, in the second half there was hardly a chance to draw breath as The Magpies blew away the best the Second Division had to offer 5-2. Quinny bagged four, what a debut! He couldn't run far but over a yard he was quicker than anybody else in the game!

Promotion or Bust

A week later, Oges and I were beating that familiar track from Preston via the M6 and A50 to Leicester. They'd gone down instead of us in 1987 and, despite being one of the division's bigger clubs, hadn't looked much like coming back up in '88 or '89. But with players like Wayne Clark (who Smith had nearly signed instead of Quinn) and the talented midfielder Gary McAllister, City were still a force to be reckoned with at this level.

In spite of going behind early on, Newcastle fought back with goals from Gallacher and Quinn to go in a goal to the good at half-time. We looked formidable going forward but Smith's United was already showing frailty in defence. The back four, Ranson, Thorn and Scott, all with bags of top-flight experience, and left-back Paul Sweeney, looked OK on paper. Yet in typical Newcastle United fashion, they were as leaky as a tea-strainer on grass. Almost inevitably Leicester gained a second-half equaliser as they laid siege to our goal and we had to go home happy with a share of the spoils. It was going to be a long, hard season in this harsh new environment of Division Two!

The following weekend Quinny was at it again, bagging both goals to secure a 2-1 home win over Joe Royle's Oldham, who were themselves a good outside bet for promotion. It had been a sound enough start to the season and I'd been able to see all three opening fixtures. However, in my absence, the next two games, away at Bournemouth and Oxford, were both disappointing 1-2 defeats. Newcastle were beginning to display a level of inconsistency that, apart from a golden spell through April, would dog them throughout the season. No sooner had they reached peak form before they would tumble all the way back to where they'd started. The next four games saw wins over Portsmouth, Watford and Hull with a 0-0 draw at Joker Park, in the first Tyne-Wear derby for 4½ years, sandwiched in between. Was the formbook about to go out of the window?

Not if almost two full halves of dreary football in the next home game against Bradford were anything to go by. The away team held out resolutely at 0-0 for the full 90 minutes. Up to then, Micky Quinn had been the pick of the new signings with an incredible 15 league goals and Mark Mc Ghee had only played a bit part in United's opening gambit. With Quinny unable to add to his total that day, many of the 20,000 fans had already passed through the exits when McGhee picked the ball up in the centre circle deep into injury time. Those of us who were left bellowed at the Scotsman to punt it forward before the referee could blow for time. He did no such thing! Instead, one by one he proceeded to take on and beat every single Bradford player until, one-on-one with the keeper, he slotted the ball into the Leazes End net. There was a mixture of euphoria and disbelief among the 15,000 or so left inside the ground and those who'd left early must have felt pissed off when they heard what they'd missed!

By now I'd left Lancashire Polytechnic with an HND in Science, having completed my studies the previous June, and I'd spent the summer living with my girlfriend Gail in Preston. It was something of an idyllic existence, out drinking with Oges every Friday night and mapping-out our plan of action for the 'Promotion Season' ahead while Gail was out with Oges' other half, Lesley. I'd been employing the rest of my time trying to find a job in industry and had finally gained success just before the Bradford game, securing a job in the labs of a polymer company in Manchester. The change from student life in Preston to a working existence in Manchester was a tough one, especially after I split with Gail not long after moving. But with one continuous thing still in my life, Newcastle United, I was able to soldier on through the adversity!

Promotion or Bust

For the time being, in the league, Newcastle continued to pick up points throughout the early autumn, in spite of going out of the League Cup early, yet again. Promotion rivals Blackburn were put to the sword, as were Brighton, before we proceeded to throw away a two-goal lead in the last ten minutes at home to plucky Port Vale. The following week, we annihilated our League Cup conquerors West Brom 5-1 at The Hawthorns, before squandering two more home points in a scrappy 2-2 draw against Middlesbrough.

Buoyed by another laudable away result, drawing 0-0 at West Ham, seven days later Oges and I made the short journey over the Pennines to Barnsley. This was the sort of away game that Second Division football was all about. A crumby football ground on top of a moor, with sheep grazing in a field behind the away end. I swear I could hear the music from the Hovis advert whistling in the teeth of the force nine gale as it ripped across the open terrace! We expected to be rewarded for our resilience with three points on the continuous march back to the top flight, especially as the previous week struggling Barnsley had been thrashed 7-0 by West Brom, the team we'd just put five past. Funny how these things never work out the way you expect! Barnsley started the game edgily but soon realised that their more expensively assembled opponents weren't at the races in the cold, blustery conditions.

After Barnsley had 'unbelievably' gone ahead just after the break, a section of the travelling support, cold, wet and completely pissed-off with the inept performance of The Magpies, decided to let a few of those they didn't consider good enough know exactly how they felt. Top of the list were the inconsistent Kevin Dillon, whose cause wasn't helped by the fact he was from Sunderland, and the consistently crap Wayne Fereday. As Newcastle desperately sought an equaliser, Fereday skewed a cross into the away section and was roundly booed. Soon after, Smith took him off, replacing him with John Anderson, an old boy popular with all Newcastle fans bar Oges. Again United pushed forward with the ball being played out to Anderson, who cut inside from his wide position and took a glance up at his options. Johnny had a bit of a shot on him and, ignoring all his better-placed colleagues, decided to have a blast for goal. He sliced his shot horribly though, and the ball swerved out for a throw-in on the far side. "OOOOH! Hard to bear, Johnny!" sympathised the Toon Army as Anderson wasted possession just as blatantly as Fereday had only minutes earlier. Oges, by contrast, was incandescent, hopping about on the damp terrace in a fit of rage, spluttering Ando's name every few seconds amongst a torrent of expletives! In spite of this latest setback, however, we were now very much in the ascendancy and eventually grabbed an equaliser from the irrepressible Quinn, ten minutes from time. Our unbeaten run was extended to eight matches, setting things up nicely for the visit of promotion rivals Sheffield United the following week.

By this time, late November, the league table was starting to sort itself out into a three horse race for the two automatic promotion places between Leeds, Newcastle and Sheffield United. The Blades, only just promoted from Division Three, were under the guidance of Dave 'Harry' Bassett and played a long ball game up to their prolific forwards Deane and Agana. Attracted by this crunch encounter, Oges and I were in the company of an old mate from Lancs. Poly, Mark, an ardent Blades fan. We escorted him to the away turnstiles in the Leazes and then made our own way into the closest section of the Milburn Paddock. This was a calculated gamble based on the hope that at half-time we would be able to goad Mark through the fence if things were going well. They did, Newcastle scoring the only two goals of the game through Gallacher and Quinny before the break, and we set about our unsporting behaviour during the interval.

"Reidy what's the score, Reidy, Reidy what's the score?" we enquired of our mate as he did his best to pretend he couldn't hear! Newcastle were now in a great position with Leeds away to come the following week.

The nine-game unbeaten run was ended with the Magpies going down narrowly 0-1 at Elland Road. We had now played our two principal rivals in three out of the four scheduled meetings and were still in contention. If we could just keep the results coming against the lesser sides we were in with a big shout. That was exactly what we couldn't do. The blip became a major wobble as we lost the next two games at home to Oxford and away at Stoke. By the time we'd been undone by a first half Steve Bull hat-trick at home to Wolves on New Year's Day, the top two were disappearing over the horizon and all hopes of automatic promotion looked sunk. Newcastle hadn't won now in five league games and The Bald Eagle decided to look to the transfer market. Signing Celtic and former Scotland midfielder Roy Aitken for £500,000, Smith gave him his debut against Leicester at St. James' on January 13th 1990.

The game began well enough and by ten minutes into the second half we were 2-1 up. Then it all started to go pear-shaped. Unexpectedly, Leicester added three more to their tally so that by the 80th minute it was 2-4! The promotion bubble seemed to have well and truly burst and Newcastle looked set to collapse into mid-table as they had from exactly the same position ten years before. Supporters streamed out of the ground, bitterly disappointed. Of the 21,000 at the start there were probably little more than half that left to see Newcastle, driven on by the never-say-die Aitken, cut the arrears to 3-4 with five minutes to go. Then, to the massive relief of all those still present, we went level in the final minute. The momentum was now well and truly with the Magpies and in injury time, Mark McGhee was about to weave his magic again. Picking the ball up on the edge of the area, he started to go on one of his runs. Standing at the opposite end of the ground in the Leazes, I just knew he was going to score as soon as he set off. McGhee played a one-two from the penalty spot and accepted the return pass on the edge of the six-yard box, stabbing the ball gleefully into the net. 5-4! Of course, the commotion was half what it would have been if the full crowd had been there but the hysteria was still something to have witnessed. There were no TV cameras to capture the comeback for posterity but anyone else who remembers that game from first hand will surely say it was equally good, if not better than, the Alan Shearer inspired 4-3 win over the same opponents some seven years later!

The emphasis was different now. Leeds and Sheffield United were too far ahead to contemplate catching them. We had to compete with the clubs around us and make sure of a place in the Football League promotion lottery, otherwise known as the play-offs. Aitken's presence was still highly influential and, in the first play-off six-pointer we faced, at Boundary Park, he inspired the side back from 0-1 down to grind out a valuable 1-1 draw on Oldham's windswept plastic pitch. Another three 1-1 draws followed, including away to Sheffield United and the return derby match at home to Sunderland. Three consecutive home wins over more lowly opposition ensured the points total kept piling up and Newcastle sat comfortably in the play-off places going into March.

Promotion or Bust

Whilst the urgent business of promotion was being attended to, we had embarked on an interesting little distraction in the FA Cup. Easy progress through the third and fourth rounds had set up a fascinating fifth round tie at home to Manchester United. They were suffering their worst season in the league for years and rumours were rife that if they didn't have a decent cup run, Alex Ferguson was going to be sacked. Their main problem was their ineffective strike force, which in a recent televised match had missed chance after chance. One crude joke circulating round Manchester at the time was that before his execution, the final wish of ousted President Ceaucescu of Romania had been to be shot by Brian McClair!

It was also an interesting time for me in my new workplace, where 50% of the workforce were City, 49% United and 1% Newcastle. At least I had the City fans on my side! Unfortunately though, the Man. United revival began the week before we were due to entertain them. The game was keenly contested, with Newcastle twice coming back from behind before succumbing to a late Danny Wallace strike. For the second time in three seasons we fell at home in round five to the eventual cup winners.

The play-off quest resumed without further ado. The next home game saw me opting for a place on the Leazes End rather than attending my cousin's wedding reception in Gosforth. Quinny made the decision worthwhile, scoring twice in a 2-1 win over Ipswich. Seven days later, I was at Ewood Park with Oges, hoping to exact some form of retribution against my ex, Gail, in the form of a victory over her hometown club. The venture was a miserable failure in every sense. Not only did we lose 0-2, we were also caught in a blizzard outside the ground after the match and almost froze to death! I've hated everything to do with Blackburn Rovers ever since.

Standing in the Corner

Following the Blackburn reverse, Newcastle embarked on a run of six consecutive victories through April. On the day of the Ewood Park game we were fourth on 57 points. When on Easter Monday we beat Stoke 3-0 at St. James' with two goals from Kristensen and one from Quinny, Newcastle stole into the second automatic promotion spot on 75 points, just ahead of Sheffield United. It had become a case of any two from three again, with us, the Blades and Leeds well clear of Swindon, Blackburn, Sunderland and Oldham, who were slugging it out for the play-offs.

By now it was late in the season and there were only four games left, two home and two away. The last match of 1989-90, at Middlesbrough, was already sold-out, so Oges and I decided to make our final away trip of the season the long haul down to Plymouth, the weekend straight after Easter. The excursion was supposed to be a long spring weekend of drink and football, but as neither of us could afford to stay down there we were forced to rationalise. It would have to be the train there and train back on the day of the match. That was no problem - after all, they sold beer on Intercitys!

The problem I hadn't foreseen was that of my four twelve-hour nightshifts, which had begun immediately on arrival back in Manchester after the Stoke game. After the last one, ending on Friday morning, I managed to grab a few hours' kip before making my way up to Preston for a traditional Friday night piss-up. But the next catch was that we had to get a train to Birmingham at 4am in order to make the Plymouth connection. As I'd slept during the day, I volunteered to stay awake and the first leg of the journey went without a hitch. Oges trudged like a zombie all the way to the railway station, muttering, "Are we really doing this?" and then snoozed for the whole two hours through to Birmingham. By the time he came round, the sun was nearly up and the Brummie nightlife was just about to close down. We asked for directions to the nearest McDonald's to get breakfast and a complete twat of a railwayman sent us right through the heart of the red light district. This forced us to run the gauntlet of scores of hookers eager to offer their services just once more before the close of trading. Worse still, just as we were recovering from a sight far worse than a Bigg Market hen party, they all descended on the takeaway and gave us the evils for spurning their propositions. We beat a hasty retreat; surely things could only get better! By the time we were en route from New Street, though, my body clock was completely shot. My brain clearly thought I was still on night-shift, but the train was busy and I couldn't get any sleep. "Only one thing for it," suggested Oges, "we'll have to start drinking beer." Great idea! It worked too - it got rid of my hangover straight away and I forgot all about my tiredness. We trooped off the train at Plymouth and immediately found a pub on the way to the ground for more beer and some lunch. I was feeling fine now. The alcohol and energy levels were back up and the adrenaline had kicked in!

The match itself was no classic. In the first half, Plymouth took the lead against the run of play only for Newcastle to reply before the break through McGhee. The news at half-time was good - Sheffield United weren't winning. The second period was uneventful except for a disallowed goal by Quinn. I was the only Newcastle supporter who hadn't seen the linesman's flag and, even though I had an excuse for being the worse for wear, I felt a bit of a prat as I was in mid-air as Quinny's volley hit the corner of the net! Fortunately, in those days, my vocal celebrations didn't start until my feet touched back down on the terrace and by then I'd realised my mistake. As the match ended 1-1, the news from Bramall Lane was even better - the Blades were a goal behind, and although this was only a latest score, we all felt confident of being a further point ahead in second place.

When we got on the train home however, the mood of everyone changed. Some lads had left the ground early and watched the final scores come in on TV in the station bar. They broke the bad news: Sheffield United had scored twice in injury time - we were down to third. The shock immediately triggered my 'shift-lag' again and no amount of beer could make me feel better this time. The journey back was pure misery, compounded by the usual British Rail excuses about signal failures. We eventually arrived back in Preston at 4am, 24 hours after we'd set off. And after all that we were back in the play-off places!

Despite only dropping two more points following Plymouth, Newcastle still needed to win the last game at Middlesbrough and hope for one of the other two to slip-up to gain automatic promotion. Three things went against us - the fact our game was a local derby, it was away and that Leeds and Sheffield United were both at home. In the end, all the permutations were rendered meaningless as Boro, needing to win to avoid relegation, hammered us 4-1. The other two had won anyway and after all the hope in April, we would have to go back to square one and fight it out in the play-offs. It was a bitter disappointment.

When all the results were in there was another shock. Newcastle had finished third on 80 points, whilst in fourth, fifth and sixth places respectively, separated only by goal difference, Swindon, Blackburn and Sunderland had all finished with 74. Therefore, under the rules of the play-offs, we would first have to defeat bitter enemies Sunderland to reach the final at Wembley. Yet another North East rival stood between Newcastle and our rightful place in Division One.

Promotion or Bust

And so, on Sunday May 13th 1990, the day after the FA Cup Final, the giants of Tyneside and Wearside locked horns in the first leg of the semi-final at Joker Park. It was a bad tempered affair with the Mackems' Paul Hardyman sent off for kicking Budgie after the Newcastle keeper had saved a penalty at the death. The second leg three days later was even worse tempered. On a miserable evening, thick drizzle oozed down the back of my collar as I stood alongside Oges in the Milburn paddock, hoping fate would belatedly deliver our just reward. The stakes couldn't be higher. Swindon, who led after the first leg of the other semi-final, had been charged with misconduct by the FA over a variety of financial irregularities. If they won the play-offs and were subsequently demoted a division as punishment (the probable outcome) the runners-up would be promoted in their place. As things stood, this game was the final. Up above us in the stand, Chris Waddle and Gazza sat, their domestic season over, killing time before the World Cup Finals in Italy. How we could have done with those two in our side. Come to think of it, if we'd still had them we wouldn't have been in this predicament - we'd never have been relegated.

The match began at a frantic pace, Newcastle trying for all their worth to break the deadlock early on. Most Newcastle fans hoped to stuff Sunderland like we had on New Year's Day 1985 and few, me included, contemplated defeat. To everyone's disbelief, though, it was Sunderland who opened the scoring against the run of play through diminutive pensioner Eric Gates. Still, there was over an hour left to get the goal back - away goals didn't count until after extra time.

In the second half, United huffed and puffed but just didn't seem able to create an opening. Time was now running out and as we pushed forward with even greater urgency, Sunderland delivered the sucker punch. Gabbiadini broke free and beat Budgie to make the score an unassailable 0-2 with only ten minutes left. The sight of Sunderland fans jumping onto the pitch from the Leazes End to mob their goalscorer gave their opposite numbers what little excuse they needed to mount a far greater pitch invasion from the Gallowgate. Such action was futile and only likely to attract tough sanctions from the FA. If the game had been abandoned, the tie would have been awarded to Sunderland anyway.

Inevitably, referee George Courtney took the players from the pitch and then stood right in front of us at the mouth of the tunnel as the police fought to clear spectators from the playing area. Courtney had an unsettling look of self-righteousness, typical of a school headmaster, and as I aimed an insult in the direction of Eric Gates, who was standing beside him, he glared directly at me. I half expected him to wave a dismissive finger as well.

"Piss off, Skeletor!" a voice from right behind me yelled, its owner noting the referee's likeness for the evil *Masters of the Universe* character and obviously thinking the initial frosty gaze was at him. Skeletor continued glowering into the paddock as though, if he concentrated hard enough, his dark powers could turn us all to stone. If he could have done, I'm sure he would. I doubt George Courtney thought highly of any football fans, but on that day I believe his particular problem was with the bad children of Tyneside!

The players did eventually return to play out the meaningless last few minutes, but the game was now up in every sense of the word for Newcastle United. The pain was unbearable. To have lost to the scum was one thing, but to have finished third, clear of the other three play-off teams by more points than we were behind the eventual champions, felt a grave injustice. Sunderland did lose to Swindon in the final but were promoted in their place anyway after the Wiltshire side's expected demotion. It was small comfort that they were immediately relegated twelve months later. Ambitious Leeds, beaten so convincingly by us on the opening day, would finish their first season back in the top flight sixth and a year after that were crowned Football League Champions. How our fortunes diverged after that glorious August day. Italia 90 was about to capture the imagination of a brand new football public, but for the Toon Army the summer of 1990 was one to forget.

Twelve

Terminal Decline?

With the burden of 30 million kettles almost fusing the National Grid, the country watched square-eyed as England took West Germany to penalties in the semi-final of Italia 90. Little did we know it but as the tearful Gazza shambled through extra time, just like at St. James' not two years before, a new era in English football was dawning. With it would come a completely new kind of football fan. Within a few years, 'soccer nuts' would be watching football matches in replica shirts and face-paint without needing to go anywhere near a football ground, courtesy of a phenomenon called Sky Sports. The beautiful game, maligned for the best part of two decades, was suddenly becoming the new rock n' roll!

It was difficult not to get carried along by all the hype. Even though the Madchester experience was at its zenith in the summer of 1990, something bigger had caught the public imagination. Every second person on every main street across the country seemed to be wearing a T-shirt with "There'll always be an England" and Gazza's bubbling mugshot emblazoned across it. Even a cynical old traditionalist like me, whose team was still imprisoned in Division Two, responded in kind. Back in the North East during my employer's summer shutdown, I blew the sum of two hundred quid on a season ticket for the benches in the East Stand Paddock. Oges, similarly inspired by this new age of football, quickly followed suit and gave

Terminal Decline?

NUFC another two hundred for the adjacent space. We had both moved up in the world, abandoning the terraces for the luxury of seating and a roof!

It was the ambition of almost all terrace dwellers at St. James' Park to spend a season on the benches. Not many envied the people of the stands their sedate existence with packed lunches and flasks, but this part of the ground was different. Who could fail to have been impressed by the fans of the East Paddock bouncing to their feet to hurl abuse at the linesman whenever he made a wrong decision? And who would wish to pass up the opportunity of throwing the ball back with venom at an opponent who'd been pissing you off for the whole game? The season to come would seem the ideal opportunity to sample life in the most exciting part of St. James' Park!

Whilst competition was likely to be stronger in 1990-91, there was to be an extra promotion place to increase the size of the top flight back up to 22 clubs. With three automatic promotion slots and one play-off place on offer, surely we couldn't miss out on a return to the Promised Land this time. It meant that everyone down to seventh in the table would be in with a shout. Sheffield Wednesday, who had traded places with their Steel City rivals on the last day of 89-90, would be the biggest threat, with West Ham likely to ask more questions than last time. Oldham, who'd enjoyed two thrilling cup-runs and only missed the play-offs by a whisker, were again the best outside bet but, once more, it was Newcastle who were installed as favourites to go up by the bookies.

For the second successive season, a magnificent 24,000 gate was present to see the opening fixture at St. James' Park and for the second time in a row, we were rewarded with a comprehensive Newcastle win. The opposition, Plymouth, was more modest than twelve months before but, nonetheless, the Toon kicked off with the sort of top-drawer performance befitting Division Two favourites. Quinn and Kristensen bagged the goals for 2-0 but it could easily have been double figures. There wasn't even the opportunity to barrack the linesman - carnival time in the East Stand Paddock was up and running!

The following week, things got even better as we beat Blackburn 1-0 away, although in circumstances far less convincing than Plymouth. The previous season's two play-off semi-finalists were heading for a dull 0-0 stalemate when, deep into injury-time, Newcastle won a corner in front of the home fans in the Blackburn End. Kevin Dillon struck the worst corner kick I've ever seen straight at the first defender but Rovers left-back Sulley, clearly thinking of his first pint in the players' lounge, could only scuff his clearance. Liam O'Brien, alert and far from intoxicated, reacted quickest and drilled the loose ball into the net. Suzanne Vega would hardly have believed it. Her acapella classic *Tom's Diner* rang around Ewood Park - the unlikeliest of tunes to assume the role of a Toon Army victory anthem!

The following Saturday, relegated Millwall, top of the First Division less than twelve months before, administered a bitter dose of reality. In front of another 24,000 gate they humbled us 1-2, knocking the wind out of all the early season confidence. My optimism wasn't going to be deflated that easily though. Following another week of nightshifts, I decided to get used to daylight again by making the short train journey from Manchester to Stoke for our next game at Port Vale.

According to a recent Granada TV sports programme, Vale Park had almost become the Wembley of the North. Using aerial photography that wouldn't have looked out of place on *Time Team*, the programme makers showed how, in the 1950s,

Malcolm MacDonald - Supermac - challenging for a header at The Gallowgate End.

Gordon Lee alongside Richard Dinnis on the bench (Lee looking suitably sinister!).

Alan Gowling shooting at goal.

**Arthur Cox receiving Manager of the Month
on the pitch.**

Kevin Keegan (as a player) scoring on his debut against QPR.

Chris Waddle playing v. Spurs (the club he was about to sign for) in 1984-85.

**Peter Beardsley shadowed by John Barnes of
Watford in 1986-87. They both signed for
Liverpool shortly afterwards.**

Jack Charlton doing a Brown Ale promotion at the pre-season photo-call, 1984-85.

Iam McFaul (as manager) on the bench
alongside his assistant (later caretaker)
Colin Suggett.

Fans clearing snow off the Gallowgate End in
the 1980's. The view is from 'the Scoreboard'
looking towards 'the Corner'.

**Gazza taking on Vinnie Jones in the
1988 FA Cup 5th Round tie.**

**Paul Goddard challenging for a cross.
(Glenn Roeder is in the background)**

**Mirandinha unable to find a way past
Wimbledon defenders on his home debut.**

John Cornwell, Gazza (on the fence) and Mirandinha celebrate. The goal was one of three against Chelsea in 1988, securing Newcastle a place in the Mercantile Football League Centenary Competition at Wembley.

**Jim Smith unveiled as the new manager
(with chairman Gordon McKeag
- Sack The Board!).**

**Mick Quinn scoring his fourth goal on his
debut against Leeds.**

The new West (soon to be Milburn) Stand on its completion in 1988.

Ossie Ardiles on the Milburn Stand Steps following his appointment, holding a Newcastle scarf aloft.

**Gavin Peacock celebrating a goal
with Lee Clark.**

David Kelly celebrating with Gavin Peacock.

Kevin Keegan (as manager - pre Premiership) on the bench with Terry Mac.

Andy Cole in action in the First Division.

**Andy Cole, Scott Sellars & Lee Clark
celebrating a goal near the end of the
First Division Championship season.**

**The ground complete for its 36,000
all-seater capacity.**

Terminal Decline?

planners had intended to erect huge stands at each end of the ground to cover the vast, over-sized kops. Where the fans to fill them were supposed to come from nobody bothered to explain. Once inside the ground, two major similarities between it and the twin towers did become apparent. Vale Park was both dilapidated and crumbling!

For the third game in a row, Newcastle put in a less than convincing performance. For eighty minutes, the Potteries side were the better team. Crucially, they lacked one thing - a natural goalscorer - and chances came and went begging, much to the relief of the three thousand Geordies thronging on the unfeasibly large terrace. It was beginning to look as if the only thing we possessed was a decent goalscorer - Micky Quinn. The rest of the team looked ordinary and, critically, those senior players brought in to achieve promotion in 1989-90 were now a year older. The previous campaign's young sensation, John Gallacher, would be out for the entire season through injury and his flair and penetration were sorely missed as 1990-91 became a bridge too far for Jim Smith's Newcastle.

At Vale Park, however, there was still some room for optimism. Having hardly been involved in the game, in the 80th minute Quinny suddenly found himself one-on-one, with Vale keeper Trevor Wood having advanced to the edge of his area. Coolly, the tubby Scouser lobbed Wood, the ball bounced once and right down in front of us the net bulged. We'd won 1-0 against the run of play for the second away game running. It'd been another great start to the season, but Newcastle would have to find some genuine form soon if it was ever going to last.

Following a fine 2-2 draw at Sheffield Wednesday in midweek, for the first twenty-five minutes of the next game at home to West Ham, the Magpies looked to be doing exactly that. One goal to the good and bossing the game, United were cruising, in constant search of a second goal and never looking like letting the Hammers back in. That was until a calamitous error by Burridge, one of several that season that would all come at crucial times. With Ranson up-field, Budgie decided to chase for a ball in the right-back position, which was running towards the corner flag and no cause for immediate danger. Having left his area, the keeper was beaten to the ball and when it was crossed back into the middle, the goal gaped for West Ham to equalise. After that disappointment, we never managed to get back into our rhythm. West Ham were happy to settle for a point from a game they'd looked like losing heavily, but for Newcastle it was a case of two more points dropped. The Magpies just seemed unable to get going and the initiative was gradually being lost.

After a 0-1 defeat at Bristol City, the prospect of three games in two weeks against Middlesbrough offered the chance to get our season back on track. The first game, a League Cup tie, first leg at Ayresome Park, ended in another defeat, 0-2, but the all-important league match at St. James' the following Wednesday was the one we regarded as most important. Boro had also started the season well and a win would equate to taking six points off them in the promotion race. In a moment of bitter irony, as I asked to take my Wednesday night-shift off as holiday, I'd predicted to my lab manager that we would draw the league game and then win the second leg the following week 1-0. How more right could I have been? Despite dominating the 90 minutes, we couldn't find a way past Boro's resolute 11-man defence. We had to settle for 0-0. The following week a meaningless 1-0 win meant that we were out of the League Cup and had only taken three points from a possible twelve. Worse still, becoming less popular by the game on Tyneside,

Terminal Decline?

habitual derby match ref Skeletor had sent off Quinny in the second leg. We would be without our talisman for a vital two matches while he served out his suspension.

Quinny signed-off before starting his ban by bagging both goals in a 2-1 home win over Portsmouth but our reliance on him was now far too great. Without Quinn, Newcastle's form took a nosedive and we claimed just three points from our next seven games, plummeting down into mid-table. At Hull City and Wolves, we were terrible, losing both games 1-2, although at unsightly Molineux at least there was a silver lining in the form of a consolation goal by 18-year-old Lee Clark. These were to be my last two away games for almost a year as, like in 1987-88, tighter cash flow forced me to rationalise. Factors leading to destitution all usually come along at once and though I wasn't sad to see the back of my night-shift duties, the return to permanent day-shift saw my salary reduced considerably. This coincided with the welcome news that the letting agency had increased the rent for my flat by 20%!

At least my home games were already paid for but others were less happy with the way Newcastle's season was going down the pan. Gates at St. James' Park were averaging less than 20,000 for the first time in nearly a decade as patchy form, home and away, through Christmas kept the Magpies well adrift of the play-offs.

What we needed was some excitement in the Cup to rekindle the hopes of the Toon Army. Four days before the third round tie at home to Derby, United had looked to be taking all three points at top of the table Oldham. Then, in the final minute, Mark Stimson had put through his own goal to gift Latics a share of the points. If Oges' bête-noir was still Johnny Anderson then everybody else's at St. James' Park was Stimson, the blonde-haired southern softy of a left-back who could do nothing right on the park for Newcastle. He'd need to do something special in the cup match to make amends for his gaffe at Boundary Park and unbelievably he did. With the Magpies leading their top-flight opponents 1-0 through a goal from Quinn and a sublime display from young Steve Watson, Stimson drove a shot low from thirty yards straight into the bottom corner of the Gallowgate End net. 2-0 - we were on our way!

Newcastle's reward was another home tie against First Division opposition, this time the much tougher Nottingham Forest. And we nearly did it again, United striding into a confident 2-0 advantage through the old deadly duo of Quinn and McGhee. The fun didn't last long this time though. Forest clawed back two goals to earn a replay at The City Ground, where brave Newcastle went down 3-0. The dream would end at Wembley for Brian Clough's Forest side but for the Magpies the season was now all but over - out of the cup and too far adrift of seventh place to maintain any realistic hope of promotion.

In late March 1991, Jim Smith stepped down as manager having failed in his quest first to maintain and then to restore Newcastle United's First Division status. In some respects, like the previous season's third place and injuries, he'd been unlucky, while in others he was clearly the architect of his own downfall.

Smith made some excellent signings but he'd also picked up some absolute lemons. Dillon, Fereday and Aitken all failed at St. James' Park following excellent careers elsewhere, while Askew, Brazil and Bradshaw never really figured in the first team picture. There had also been another casualty of Newcastle's disappointing season. With the Magpie Group now holding the majority of shares, John Hall had joined the board in the previous close season and quickly

Terminal Decline?

pushed through his plans for a share issue. The flotation was launched in late autumn but coincided with the team's slump into mid-table and insufficient applications for shares were received. The venture was disappointingly scrapped, but fortunately for the Toon Army, John Hall did not walk away and launched a new campaign to take control of the club from within.

The Bald Eagle's replacement was Ossie Ardiles, taken from Swindon whom he'd steered to play-off victory the previous season before their demotion. His brief was to build a team around the crop of promising youngsters he had at his disposal and make a push for promotion the following year. After Newcastle went down 0-2 at home to Bristol Rovers on April Fools' Day, Ardiles summarily declared the play-offs out of reach. At least the 17,500 fans that braved that miserable defeat had something to cheer before the end. When Mark Stimson careered in for his second crude challenge of the afternoon, the referee must have thought he was hearing things as he reached into his pocket. All around St. James' Park there were chants of "OFF! OFF! OFF!" followed by a loud cheer when the red card was produced! Even in the depths of despair we could still have a laugh at our own expense.

After a 0-3 mauling at the hands of Neil Warnock's Notts County, the Second Division's surprise package in 90-91, Ardiles inspired Newcastle to back-to-back home victories over promotion-chasing Oldham and Sheffield Wednesday. It was only a brief flurry however and we then failed to win any of our last six games to finish a depressing eleventh. With the usual mob of high-spirited one-match-a-season fans descending on St. James' for the last game, you'd have thought it was a promotion party we were attending, not a 1-2 defeat at the hands of relegated Hull. Nevertheless, there was one glimmer of hope for the future in the form of a superb goal by Lee Clark. It was a classic turn and

Standing in the Corner

strike from the edge of the Gallowgate End penalty area, reminiscent of so many scored in similar fashion by Paul Gascoigne in better times. How long ago those glory days seemed now. And how long would it be before we tasted the sweetness of top-flight football again?

During the summer of 1991, having long pondered my future in Manchester and having chased every job opportunity that came up back in Preston and the North East, something happened to change my mind. A work colleague, who'd heard that I used to play bass in a part-time blues band at Lancs. Poly, came up with an offer. His mate was the drummer of a ska band and they were looking for a new bass player.

Was I interested? What the hell! I gave it a go and lo and behold, two years after jacking my 'music career' in, I landed a gig in Manchester's foremost two-tone band, Bezeteran Blue.

The change to my lifestyle was phenomenal and immediate. Having often had nothing to do other than work in between my visits to St. James' Park and up to Preston for the odd Friday night out, I was now attending twice weekly band practises and gigging all round Greater Manchester. Something would have to give and in what became a hectic schedule, that something was inevitably the Magpies. I couldn't afford to renew my season ticket anyway and with gigs and practises frequently falling on Saturday, for the first time in six seasons I was reduced to the status of a part-time supporter. In the following season, the worst in the history of Newcastle United, I made it to only ten games as I had to cherry-pick from the few weekends I had free. Some may think that a season 'lost' would be worth it for the sake of living the life of a budding rock-star. Not me! Psychologically, it was one of the worst years of my life and I put that as much down to missing the weekly routine I'd enjoyed so much for the

Terminal Decline?

last six years as the stress of trying to cope with two full-time occupations. I found out for the one and only time that I was unable to survive without my minimum twice-weekly fix of NUFC! I've never tried it again since.

Ardiles made only minor changes to the playing staff in preparation for that fateful 1991-92 campaign as, for the most part, the emphasis was going to be on the youth already at the club. Out went old-stagers Aitken, McGhee and Anderson, who'd been granted his testimonial. In their place came young but experienced replacements. Franz Carr, who'd shown signs of becoming the new John Robertson early in his career at Forest, was acquired to provide the penetration sadly lacking the season before. Attacking midfielder Gavin Peacock arrived from Bournemouth and before the season was three months old, striker David Kelly was signed for £250,000 from Leicester. There were a legion of youngsters included in the first team squad and, even allowing for the experience elsewhere in the team, it was just too much to expect so many of them to cut it at senior level. Apart from the established Clark, Watson and Steve Howey (then a forward), David Roche, Matty Appleby, Robbie Elliot, Alan Thompson and Lee Makel all saw service in the first team which now operated with Ardiles' much vaunted diamond system in midfield.

Early form was patchy rather than an ominous sign of things to come. All the opening month and a half confirmed was that we still weren't good enough to stand any chance of promotion. In the first week of September, Newcastle renewed their acquaintance with Stokesy's Tranmere Rovers at Prenton Park and I was able to see at first hand the mess Ossie's emphasis on youth had made of the team. United were diabolical and only through outrageous fortune did we go in 2-1 up at half-time. Tranmere, promoted through the play-offs the season before, were easily the better side and the Magpies' comeuppance was inevitable. Ten minutes into the second half, after sustained pressure by the home team, new Czech keeper Pavel Srnicek advanced out of his area to clear up-field but only succeeded in driving the ball onto the shins of closing Rovers striker Ian Muir. The ball cannoned back over Pav's head and into the empty net. After that, there was only ever going to be one outcome and Newcastle did well to keep the score down to 2-3, sparing me little embarrassment at the hands of my mate yet again!

The rest of September and early October was a miserable time as we lost four more games and took just two points from home draws with Ipswich and Derby. The only win in the sequence was a bizarre 4-3 League Cup success over Third Division Crewe at Gresty Road, a game the Railwaymen had led 3-0 after 20 minutes. Another even more bizarre cup match occurred soon after, which involved yet another visit to Prenton Park, this time in the Zenith Data Systems (Full Members') Cup. This match was no one-sided affair. Far from it; first Tranmere had the lead, then Newcastle. The lead changed hands no fewer than four times, as by the end of extra-time the game finished 6-6 and was decided in Rovers' favour on penalties. The Zenith Cup was a fledgling Sky Sports' debut competition coverage, and the fact that the game was being televised live was a mere coincidence! High-scoring games, contrived or otherwise, would be a feature of Newcastle's season and in almost every one we would come out second best.

By the time Christmas came, trouble was looming. Home wins over Leicester, Oxford, Grimsby and Southend had kept the relegation gremlins from the door up to now but the storm clouds were finally gathering. Back home in the North East over the festive period, I was at St. James' to see a derby reverse at the hands of Boro and a much-needed 2-1 win over Bristol

Terminal Decline?

City. This was followed by an embarrassing 0-4 New Year's Day debacle at Southend. In the league, problems were really stacking up now but at least there was the annual distraction of the Cup to look forward to.

The New Year's festivities that year had a more profound effect than usual on my health. Instead of the customary headache and delicate tummy, I'd woken up to the first daylight of 1992 with a combined throat and chest infection. It put me out of action for the remaining two working days of that week, as well as forcing me to have to sit out band practise on Saturday 4th January. Out of adversity came unexpected opportunity. Feeling much better than I had the previous day, on Friday I phoned Oges to tell him I was up for the trip down to Bournemouth for the third round tie the next day - FA Cup therapy. It would greatly aid my recovery!

It was a long journey down there, of course, but much easier now the new M40 and upgraded A34 were open between Birmingham and Oxford. If only the cup tie had gone as smoothly as that journey. We and the other 2,000 Mags were rewarded for our trek with an uninspiring 0-0 draw. So it was back to Newcastle for another try on the night of January 14th, when the fog on the Tyne was at its thickest in living memory. Despite both goalkeepers' inability to see one another, the game inexplicably went ahead as twenty-two players and three officials blundered around the pitch in the pea-souper until the game was inevitably abandoned after only a quarter of an hour. It meant, of course, that there was no refund for the 20,000 fans that showed up but, in true Tyneside FA Cup tradition, a magnificent 26,000 gate was present for the re-arranged replay a week later. If it had been 26,000 neutrals, then every one would have had value for money in spite of the previous week's debacle. The game ended a thrilling 2-2 after extra-time and under brand new competition rules, we now faced our second penalty shoot-out of the season to decide the tie. Needless to say, as always, United lost the shoot-out and fell at the first hurdle yet again.

By now Newcastle were bottom of Division Two and Ardiles was drinking at the last chance saloon. The Saturday before the completed Bournemouth replay, Newcastle had done 'a Crewe', throwing away a three-goal lead to go down 3-4 at home to Charlton. On a miserable Monday morning following yet another Magpies reverse at Oxford on the first weekend in February, I was called into the office of the Technical Manager on his first day back after a trip to America. Was I about to get a dressing down for not coming to work for two days when I'd been fit enough to go all the way to the south coast for a football match? The company took a dim view of that sort of thing. But I needn't have worried; it turned out to be somebody else who was getting fired!

"Sit down, Pete," said Keith Symons, the likable Liverpudlian boss. "I thought you'd like to know, Radio Five just reported that Newcastle have sacked Ossie Ardiles. They're holding a press conference in a few minutes to announce a replacement. You'll probably want to hear what they're going to say."

He switched on his radio and immediately I heard the unmistakable Ashington accent of John Hall, now club chairman, addressing the assembled media scrum. "Thank you all for coming at such short notice... I'd like to introduce you to the new manager of Newcastle United Football Club: KEVIN KEEGAN."

"F***ing Hell!" I blurted out, realising too late that you shouldn't really swear in your manager's office! Good job he was also a football fan with a sense of humour! A few hours later I got a phone call from Oges to say he'd bought two tickets in the East Stand for the

Terminal Decline?

coming Saturday's home match with Bristol City. But I had arrangements; the band was practising on Saturday. Stuff it, this time it was far too important to miss for their sake - I was going!

Thirteen

The Second Coming

So, The Messiah was back and we would definitely need a miracle if Newcastle were to avoid the unthinkable and drop into Division Three for the first time ever. The position we found ourselves in was not dissimilar to that of February 1987, albeit a division lower. The once-proud Magpies were bottom of the table and, despite the fact that only a few points covered the bottom six sides, we'd played a game more than all our rivals. It was clear what was needed; Newcastle, without a victory in the six games played so far in 1992, had to get back into the habit of winning and fast!

The board, now dominated by the colossal presence of John Hall, had taken a massive gamble in appointing Kevin Keegan as the man to get United out of its predicament. In spite of his titanic reputation as a player and of superman standing in the eyes of the Toon Army, he'd been out of the game for eight years and possessed absolutely no coaching or managerial experience whatsoever. Since that unforgettable evening in 1984 when he ascended into lucrative tax exile in his helicopter, King Kev had been residing quietly in Spain bringing down his golf handicap. As the Gallowgate train careered off the rails under the stewardship of Ossie, the saviour of St. James' circa 1984 was conveniently in England helping with events ironically marking the Magpies' centenary year. With Ardiles unable to halt the slide, Hall concluded that

The Second Coming

Keegan was the only man with the motivational skills needed if we were to get out of the mess we were in. Without a moment's thought, KK accepted the challenge.

The stakes couldn't be higher. John Hall had predicted that the club, crippled by debts from the Milburn Stand, would fold if relegation became a reality. He of all people ought to have known. He'd stated, "The financial position is such that I couldn't sit on the sidelines any longer," as upon becoming club chairman he'd underwritten the debt by effectively making Newcastle United a subsidiary of Cameron Hall plc. In order for Hall to secure the future of the club on a permanent basis, his new manager would have to save Newcastle from disaster on the pitch, starting in earnest with the match against Bristol City.

The return of the king had an immediate effect on attendances at St. James' Park. Having dwindled to an average of 17,000 during Ardiles' tenure, 29,250 fans descended on the ground for Keegan's first match in charge. The Keegan era dawned with a convincing 3-0 win through a brace of goals from Kelly and one by O'Brien. And in a moment of pure theatre, Keegan and his swiftly recruited assistant Terry McDermott leapt from the bench to celebrate the opening goal. Snapped by the battery of photographers camped alongside the dugout rather than behind the goal, the next day Newcastle United were the subject of every back page feature, this time for all the right reasons. The recovery bandwagon was rolling. Could it gather enough momentum to escape the clutches of relegation in the weeks ahead?

Initially, the answer was yes. Following a 1-3 defeat at promotion-chasing Blackburn the week after his first game, Keegan's Newcastle won three, drew one and lost only once in the next five games, culminating in a 3-1 victory over Swindon at St. James'. By the final whistle of the Swindon match, relegation worries were almost banished, as goals from Peacock, Kelly and Quinn buried the eighth-placed Wiltshire side. Then, tuning in to Radio Five's Sports Report in the car home, a bombshell was dropped. Keegan had quit in the tunnel after the game. No reasons were initially given as to why but it was believed to have something to do with unrequited transfer money. The familiar sound of behind the scenes squabbling over finances had returned to haunt Newcastle at just about the worst possible time.

The monetary side of Keegan's survival package was a thorny issue and the little man had been known to make far-reaching decisions on matters of principal before. His first action in the transfer market had been to bring in experienced centre-half Brian Kilcline to partner Kevin Scott and Everton winger Kevin Sheedy on a free. Keegan insisted the board had promised him further money for signings but John Hall still lacked complete control of the club and was inclined to reticence wherever possible. Fortunately Hall realised Keegan was serious, so the extra cash was found and by Monday morning, King Kev and Terry Mac were back behind their desks in the Milburn Stand. A further four points were secured from the next two games and as Sunderland were slain at St. James' Park on Sunday March 29th, spring appeared to herald a much brighter future. With seven games left, we were now climbing the table away from danger and Keegan appeared to have saved Newcastle with time to spare.

Now seemed like a good time to take in another away game, so together with Oges, I made the relatively short journey to Wolves only two days after the Sunderland win. Despite the fact it was a pleasant spring evening, there were inevitable delays on the M6 north of Birmingham, and we listened to the relentless torrent of

The Second Coming

electioneering on the radio in the grim realisation that we were going to be late for the kick-off. All Radio Five wanted to talk about was politics, as pundits predicted the closest General Election for a generation. Hadn't they noticed Newcastle United's inspirational climb away from impending doom, surely the most significant news event of the past two months?

Parking near Molineux wasn't going to be easy either and, as we briskly made the ten minute walk to the ground, we heard first one roar, then a second coming from the direction of the ground. S**t! When we finally arrived, fifteen minutes into the game, Wolves were already 2-0 up through goals from Andy Mutch and Newcastle, for the first time under Keegan, disintegrated into a rabble before our eyes. By half-time, it was 4-0 and although there was a brief second half rally to reduce the arrears to just two goals, Wolves soon reassumed complete control. A fifth goal five minutes from time saw Oges and myself heading for the exit to beat the post-match rush. As we walked through the deserted street behind the large crescent-shaped stand, a loud snarl from the home fans followed by "OFF, OFF, OFF...." came rushing through the open turnstiles. Quinny, despite getting his name on the scoresheet, was having a terrible game and had resorted to kicking Wolves players to relieve his frustration, earning himself a booking just before their fifth goal. We dashed in expecting to see Quinn receive his marching orders but the ref only issued a final warning and Andy Mutch shaped up to take the resultant free kick twenty yards out. Obliged to take a seat by a zealous steward, we watched in further dismay as Wolves' number 10 curled a shot into the top corner, 6-2. Rather than being another game on the revival trail, it had been a rout and we'd had to witness the final humiliation surrounded by Wolves fans!

Standing in the Corner

We lost the next four games on the spin, including a controversial 1-4 reverse at Derby, in which referee Brian Coddington sent off three Newcastle players, Brock, Scott and O'Brien, to the fury of King Kev. The slide seemed terminal and with only two games left, at home to Portsmouth and away to fourth place Leicester, we were back in the bottom three and in need of another miracle.

Band commitments denied me the opportunity to see either of these two games, potentially the most glorious or last-ever Newcastle United fixtures. I was getting mightily p***ed-off with their non-football ways. They were probably equally p***ed-off with me constantly tuning-in nervously to Radio Five at practices, my incessant desire to go to matches and the 'scams' I pulled to achieve that goal every Saturday in eight! I wasn't going to succeed this time though, as the Portsmouth game fell on the day of a gig and we were supposed to be in a recording studio the whole weekend of the last match at Filbert Street.

I walked round with a cloud over my head for the whole afternoon of Saturday April 25th as Bezeteran Blue went about the business of setting-up and soundchecking at The Lancaster Tavern in Manchester. My trusty radio was tuned in, as always to 693AM, as I listened for news from St. James' Park. We needed to win, of course, so the silence was deafening as no reports of any goal action came out of Tyneside for over ninety minutes after three o'clock. Then at last...

"Reports of a goal coming in from St. James' Park. David Kelly, 1-0 Newcastle!"

The pint I'd been nervously drinking (fortunately from a plastic glass) flew into the air and before it could hit the ground, I'd covered fifteen yards in four seconds and was outside the front door of the pub jumping around like a lunatic, punching the air and screaming.

144

The Second Coming

Cars negotiating their way through the city centre rush hour screeched to a halt as a deranged lunatic danced about in the middle of the road! Fortunately the police weren't passing by at the time! Portsmouth down; now just Leicester to beat and we were safe!

The game down at Filbert Street presented an even greater conundrum, as my radio was banned from the recording studio. Quickly I hit on an idea. If I could get my basslines recorded promptly in the morning, there would be no need for me to be there later in the day. The rest of the tracks could be laid down over the top without me even being present. I practised conscientiously and, come Saturday morning, it all went like a dream. I was free, but there was still no time to get down to Leicester for the match. Instead, I'd arranged to meet some mates at Old Trafford cricket ground, where Lancashire were playing Hampshire in the Benson & Hedges Cup. There I could do my best to relax in a proper sporting environment, whilst keeping up to date with the score from Filbert Street in the bookies situated inside the ground.

As the clock ticked past three, I tried to take my mind off Newcastle while Lancs went about their task, restricting the visitors to 160 for 8 inside the allotted 50 overs. It was no good though, half a mile away at the more famous Old Trafford arena, Man United were playing their last home game of the season against Spurs and the crowd noise was a constant reminder of more important events far away. I lasted to 3.45 before a lull in the noise and the distant sound of tannoy announcements let me know it was time to go to Ladbrokes and find out the half-time score at Leicester.

As I entered the bookies the monitor screen marked "Half-Times" had just flicked to Division Four. The wait for the news, good or bad, felt like an eternity as the screen flicked right through the Scottish Leagues and

Standing in the Corner

back to Division One. It reminded me of what it had been like all those years before, waiting for the score to come through on the teleprinter on *Grandstand*! Then at last: Division Two. The news was good, we were winning 1-0 and other results were also going our way. I breathed a huge sigh of relief and headed to the bar to buy a round of drinks.

The second half proved even more difficult to keep out of my thoughts. Twice I went back to the bookies to check on the score, still 1-0. Eventually I couldn't stand it any longer and took my pint and paper, deserting my mates to take up permanent residence in the betting shop. The manager kindly set the monitor to show just Division Two until our score flashed up as a result and I sat trying to read, whilst glancing up at the screen every few moments. Each time it still said 1-0. By now it was getting tantalisingly close to 4.45. I glanced up once more, comforted by the familiar pixels, then looked again more urgently. Oh f***... 1-1! Suddenly, I felt close to suicide, unable to think calmly enough to look at the other scores, which would have reassured me that 1-1 was sufficient. Plummeting deeper into depression, I glanced up at the screen again: Leicester 1 Newcastle 2 (Result). It took a moment for this new information to register and then bang! For the second week in a row I made an idiot of myself, the only bloke in the bookies without a bet on whooping and screaming like I'd just won a fortune!

The rest of the cricket match was one gigantic piss-up, the Old Trafford paperseller getting to know me like a personal friend, I passed him that many times on the way to and from the bar. Hampshire's star batsman Robin Smith was fielding on the boundary right in front of us as Lancs, now batting, piled on the runs. But, for some reason, he seemed more concerned about our drinking than his team's inevitable defeat.

The Second Coming

"Whin aere yoo going too sterp?" inquired the England test player in an inquisitive South African accent.

"Never!" I replied, drunkenly. "Newcastle are staying up!"

"Gerd! Will-dern!" replied Smithy, retreating a few yards further infield.

Quite! It was a warm sunny evening, the beer was flowing and Newcastle United had avoided relegation. Three reasons to be cheerful and enjoy life!

Fourteen

The Only Way Is Up!

It was strangely coincidental that for the last ten years, every major change in my life had been mirrored by a parallel shift in the fortunes of Newcastle United. Could it be that, as once more I took my future into my own hands, the ailing Magpies were also heading for healthier times ahead?

The summer of 1992 saw me bid farewell to two of the things that had felt increasingly like millstones round my neck in the past couple of years. I'd again become convinced that my future lay away from the job I'd now been doing for three years in Manchester and had secured a place on a one year fast-track Degree course at Sheffield Polytechnic. This, in turn, had given me the excuse I'd been looking for to quit the band. That lot had cost me far too much in the way of missed football in the past twelve months and it was now time to choose the hobby I loved most - and ditch the other.

Newcastle had already moved up in the world. At the start of 1992-93, we found ourselves 'promoted' to Division One of the Football League, in spite of having finished no higher than twentieth in Division Two in the preceding campaign. Strangely enough, so had the rest of the division, except for Ipswich, Middlesbrough and Blackburn, who had all disappeared into the newly-formed FA Carling Premiership.

This new elite tier of English football immediately attracted criticism from certain sections of the media, most notably the *Daily Mirror*, who referred to it as "the greed is good league". Their viewpoint surprisingly found support in the guise of Bob Murray, chairman of Sunderland, who said his club would boycott the new structure if they got promoted and called on other Division One clubs to do likewise. John Hall was not of the same opinion though, calling the Premiership "the only place to be" and stating that it was Newcastle's aim to get there as soon as possible. Murray, a man of principle, was, however, almost as good as his word. Sunderland stayed out of the new top division for seven seasons out of the next twelve and were honest enough to drop back into the Football League at the first attempt after 'accidentally' getting promoted in 1996!

John Hall's hopes of an early elevation to Premier League status were delivered a massive boost when, at the end of 91-92, Kevin Keegan agreed to stay on as manager, together with his able assistant Terry Mac. Keegan hadn't automatically remained, of course, he'd been persuaded to by the board, now completely monopolised by former members of the Magpie Group. And, as with the one-year extension to his playing contract into the 1983-84 promotion season, there were strings attached. Money for new signings was demanded and during the close season KK gave the first indications of what would become his sublime judgement in the transfer market.

The first signing cost just £250,000 and, despite missing much of the early part of 92-93 through injury, would become an integral part of the United midfield in the latter stages. Paul Bracewell made the short journey from Joker Park, presumably unimpressed by the fact his ex-chairman's principals stood in the way of him ever playing top flight football again. Bracewell's move would reap the benefits he clearly desired and, in the autumn of his career, the influence he had on the Magpies' midfield would last fully three seasons.

Standing in the Corner

Two full-backs quickly followed onto the Keegan shopping list, both ultimately rued by a Liverpool side now ailing under the guidance of Graeme Souness. Barry Venison, like Brace a former Mackem, had been a lynchpin of Kenny Dalglish's Anfield side but now found himself surplus to requirement under the new boss. At least KK, himself a famous former Red, knew the No.2 was no donkey. As quickly as you could say "Dobbin", Keegan enticed him with the carrot of a guaranteed place in the NUFC first eleven and Venison became a Magpie. On the opposite side, at left-back, United acquired the services of John Beresford, who'd been a star of Portsmouth's impressive 1992 Cup run. Bez had been the unfortunate player who missed the deciding penalty in their semi-final replay against Liverpool. But the Reds had still been sufficiently impressed to try to lure him to Merseyside during the summer. Everything was going to plan until Beresford failed a medical and, as the deal fell through, Keegan swooped and snapped-up one of the best players ever to wear the No.3 shirt for Newcastle.

Further signings would follow later in the season and all would have as big an impact on United's future, both immediate and for seasons to come. For the time being though, all that remained for Keegan to do was persuade the influential Gavin Peacock to put pen to paper and commit himself to an extended contract at St. James' Park. This was no mean feat, as Peacock was highly coveted and already being lured, under freedom of contract, by Premiership new boys Boro. But Gav, a committed Christian, was above temptation and in any case knew better than to sign for a horde of sulphur-wheezing goblins! Keegan retained his midfield talisman for a crucial extra year. The squad was ready for business.

The new season opened with a hard-earned 3-2 home win over Southend. It was a case of another

The Only Way Is Up

home game missed for me but this year it was going to be the exception rather than the rule. Come the following Wednesday night, I was back in my rightful place in The Corner to see Newcastle beat Mansfield 2-1 in the League Cup, an uninspiring performance that belied the brilliant form waiting just around the corner. Far from stalling after initially flattering to deceive, as in 90-91, Keegan's Newcastle soon blasted into top gear and simply blew away everything that got in their way from mid-August through to the last week in October.

The highlights were numerous, as those of us who knew better struggled to comprehend such awe-inspiring league form. 2-1 revenge at Derby was sweet and in those opening weeks maximum home points were also taken from the two sides that would eventually finish second and third in the division. West Ham and Julian Dicks were sent packing 2-0 and a fortnight later Portsmouth were overpowered, 3-1. A case of win your home games at all costs - a point lost on Graham Taylor's England as they simultaneously stuttered towards World Cup qualification failure against Norway and Holland.

By the time we faced Bristol City on September 19th, Newcastle United were unstoppable. The Magpies had been inspirational in beating Portsmouth the previous weekend and we'd needed to be. Against City, an at times workmanlike performance still condemned the hapless Robins to a 5-0 drubbing. An O'Brien thunderbolt, two dubious penalties converted by Peacock, a Ronaldinho-like cross-cum-shot from Franz Carr and a late strike from Brock completed the rout in the pouring rain. It proved United were now capable of burying weak opposition even when we weren't on song. The start was now seven straight league wins, with everyone beginning to wonder when they'd wake-up and find it had all been a dream!

Standing in the Corner

Attention briefly turned to the League Cup, in which Newcastle had been drawn, over two legs, against Middlesbrough. Here was a chance to see just how good Keegan's side were against one of the teams promoted automatically the season before. And they didn't disappoint. Despite being held 0-0 after throwing everything at Boro in the first leg at St. James', United went and did it the hard way, outclassing the smoggies again on their own ground for a magnificent 3-1 win. David Kelly, with two goals, had been the star of that inspiring team performance at Ayresome Park and was finding the net regularly in the league as well. He scored in both wins either side of the Boro triumph, 2-1 at Brentford and 1-0 at home to chasing Tranmere. As 'Ned' made sure of the three points against Rovers, ending up in the back of the Gallowgate End net with the ball after heading in O'Brien's cross, Newcastle moved onto 30 points. Ten wins from ten games. Even the most pessimistic observer had begun to realise that this was no fluke and as the Geordie bandwagon gathered pace, there were ever-increasing numbers eager to jump on board.

'Making sure you got in' became something of an art form; late arrival was no longer an option for any league game. In fact "arrive early" was becoming the key phrase, as for the Tranmere game there were 30,000 inside the ground and an estimated 7,000 locked outside, with the last turnstiles having been closed an hour before kick-off. An intimate knowledge of the whole ground became a distinct advantage and I watched most of that glorious season from the Leazes and West Stand Paddocks. Somehow, the turnstiles at that end of the ground were always less busy and the last to close. Perhaps many of the 'newcomers' didn't know their way round or that there were even any turnstiles there!

The Only Way Is Up

Now the unstoppable promotion bandwagon headed for Wearside and Joker Park, which had remained unconquered by any visiting Newcastle side since 1956. Could the Toon Army clinch their eleventh astonishing straight win at the home of the enemy? The answer was a less than emphatic "yes" but the goal that clinched the most treasured win of the run was worthy of any record-breaking occasion. Liam O'Brien's 76th minute free kick, curled meticulously over and round the Sunderland wall, is most people's abiding memory of the glory that was 1992-93. The 2-1 win was hardly convincing but the outcome - Newcastle's 100% record still intact, top of the league and already 22 points clear of the scum - had all but erased the bitter memories of the play-offs two and a half years earlier. Newcastle were already a league apart from Sunderland and would remain so for most of the next decade. What a perfect way to seal eleven wins out of eleven.

All good things must come to an end eventually and it was a player ironically named Dobbin who put a stop to Newcastle's fabulous run. Grimsby Town, through the endeavours of their hard-working No.6, brought the magnificent eleven-win sequence to an abrupt and unexpected halt, leaving the Magpies beaten but still nine points clear at the top of Division One. Indeed, we had taken more points in those first twelve games than in the whole of the first thirty matches of the season before, the period before Keegan arrived. It was the end of part one of the promotion drive, the lightning start, and the beginning of the long hard winter grind where the chasing pack would have to be kept at bay.

The shock of the Grimsby reverse inevitably sparked a slight wobble. United lost successive away matches, going out of the League Cup at Chelsea 1-2 and down by the same scoreline at Leicester. Unlike in previous campaigns, however, this hiccup didn't prove any more than a minor blip and when winning ways were quickly restored, it was done in a manner for which Newcastle United would soon become famous. On a cold November evening, St. Andrew's was the venue for a game that was both bizarre and entertaining from the word go. As early as the third minute there was an incident, as United keeper Tommy Wright picked up an injury serious enough for him to eventually have to be replaced. On eight minutes, Peacock opened the scoring, only for Birmingham's David Speedie to equalise two minutes later. After half an hour Kevin Scott restored our lead but again it only lasted two minutes. Then finally, just before the interval, Franz Carr forced Matthewson to put through his own goal and send the black and whites in 3-2 ahead.

Keegan replaced the crocked Wright with Kevin Brock at half-time, relying on the veteran midfielder's amateur cricketing skills as the way to keep Birmingham out in the second half. But within three minutes of the restart, he too was the worse for injury, wobbling round punch drunk after taking a blow to the head in a goalmouth meleé. The response of the outfield players to this latest setback was consummately professional. They played immaculate possession football for the whole 45 minutes to restrict the home side to only a couple of shots on Brock's goal. The unlikely scenario of a goalless second half delivered three more away points United's way and we were back on the charge towards that Premiership Holy Grail.

By now my own toils in self-promotion were starting to bear fruit. The work for my Degree was hard but like the Mighty Magpies' efforts on the pitch the rewards were already evident in the nine-month slog towards a new beginning. My ambitions broadly matched those of Newcastle. A first, the equivalent of a major trophy, would have been nice but was, realistically, well

The Only Way Is Up

beyond my capabilities. My hope was for a 2.1 (the First Division Championship) but early results, bogged down by the fact I'd been out of higher education for four years, suggested that a 2.2 (automatic promotion) was more likely. At least I was well clear of a third (the play-offs)! In any case, student life was certainly more fun than the last eighteen months in Manchester had been, especially as unlike at Preston, I had the benefit of three years' work behind me and the monetary benefit that it conferred.

The financial dividend of United's hyperactive start to 1992-93 had seen the board honour another commitment to Kevin Keegan. They'd promised to stump-up further cash for team-building and, as the season rolled-on through November, KK invested £700,000 for another inspired signing, Charlton winger Robert Lee. Arguably Keegan's best signing of all, Lee was to be instrumental in the continued drive towards promotion, and his ability to play both wide right and in central midfield gave the squad still greater dimensions. His arrival effectively spelt the end of Franz Carr's first team existence at Newcastle, a fate that had already befallen Ranson, Quinn and Stimson in the early part of the season. As new signings continued to arrive with the efficiency of a production line, over the oncoming months a similar destiny awaited many other players who didn't figure in the Messiah's long-term strategy.

The Magpie's relentless progress continued unabated throughout the long winter months. Two more great away wins, at Charlton and Notts County, followed the Birmingham success, Watford were beaten 2-0 at St. James' Park and in another home triumph, a Ned Kelly hat-trick condemned Cambridge 4-1. Even a rare 0-1 reverse at Barnsley - another handy away game for me from my new base - couldn't dent the team's brimming confidence. Newcastle just steamrollered on through Christmas, a customary defeat at Oxford aside, picking up vital points and starting another interesting cup run with the 4-0 demolition of Port Vale.

The cup run was, on the face of it, of far greater importance than the meaningless stroll to round five it would appear. It coincided, through February, with United's only period of stuttering league form and served to keep a semblance of winning order going through an almost interminable sequence of draws. The run also provided me with another windfall of an away game at Rotherham, although getting to the tie wouldn't be as easy as the straightforward five-mile journey it looked. I hadn't got a ticket, meaning that I'd have to go there in the hope of finding somebody with one they wanted to sell. The problem of touts and match tickets vastly exceeding face value wasn't likely to be an issue for Rotherham United v Newcastle! But what was an issue was that South Yorkshire Police had decided to throw a 'ring of steel' around Millmoor to prevent any away fan not in possession of a valid ticket from getting within a quarter of a mile of the ground. Was my plan about to be thwarted? Not likely - having a little knowledge of the locality, I was aware that Millmoor, like most other Yorkshire football grounds, was situated in a residential district. No-one with 'lawful reason' to enter the area could be turned away by the police - only someone daft enough to advertise themselves as a football supporter by turning up ticketless and in full colours! Having even brushed up on my Yorkshire accent, my plan proceeded faultlessly as I slipped through the cordon without hindrance and quickly obtained a ticket for the away end. My luck was in! On the pitch though, all the good fortune went with the lucky Millers. Newcastle, at 1-0, had a goal that should have stood disallowed just before half-time. Then, on 63 minutes, Rotherham's Dean Barrick curled an indirect free kick onto Pavel Srnicek's right-hand post and the rebound dropped nicely for Nigel Johnson to equalise! Had the initial shot gone straight in, of course, the goal wouldn't have counted. Newcastle held on and won the replay, eventually going out to a last minute goal by Roy Wegerle in the fifth round at Blackburn. Then, like in 1990, the cup run gave rise to some sparkling football going into April.

The end of the FA Cup for Newcastle saw the resumption of championship form in the league. A valuable point gained at the home of principal rivals West Ham was followed by resounding victories, 3-0 at Tranmere and a 5-1 thumping of Brentford at St. James'. The win over The Bees was particularly poignant, as making his debut for the West London outfit was none other than Paul Stephenson. It was Stephenson, remember, who'd bailed out of the sinking Newcastle United ship in the desperate times of late 1988, stating as his reason a need for a more fashionable club (Millwall!) to aid his international prospects. How both parties' fortunes had changed! Such outgoing transfers were now a thing of the past, only players surplus to requirement were obliged to seek the St. James' Park exit. In the last twelve months, the revolving door in the Milburn Stand had seen a staggering improvement in the playing staff. And the unprecedented dealings of 92-93 were about to get even more remarkable.

As deadline day loomed, Keegan went back into the transfer market for the last time before the club's destiny would be decided. And if the £700,000 signing of ace left-winger Scott Sellars was indication of Newcastle's new-found ambition, then the last piece in the Gallowgate jigsaw would be so mind-blowing as to be of almost equal significance as the initial eleven-win start! Newcastle paid Bristol Rovers a record £1.75 million for striker Andy Cole and Coley would repay just about every penny with his end of season return of twelve league goals from just eleven first team starts.

Standing in the Corner

The board at United now possessed the financial clout to underwrite their championship ambitions with the sort of cash outlay that would bring tears to the eyes of their thrifty predecessors. And with sell-out crowds descending on St. James' Park for every home match, the situation had become everything they'd predicted when they launched their campaign five years before. Now, having already kept their promise to rebuild the team, they set about fulfilling their legally-binding obligation to bring the stadium into the late twentieth century. As 1992-93 entered the final straight, steel girders appeared behind the Leazes End, forming into an angled structure that quickly took on the appearance of another new stand. It certainly looked impressive as it climbed steadily into the sky, forming, at last, a link between the modern East and West Stands.

The Magpies were not now going to be denied either automatic promotion, or the championship for that matter, and United cruised down the finishing straight taking 26 from a possible 39 points after Brentford. It was too much for the chasing West Ham and Portsmouth to cope with and by the time we completed the double over Sunderland, 1-0, Newcastle required just two more points from our last three games to clinch the league crown. That requirement was duly met on the evening of May 4th at Blundell Park, Grimsby, as goals from Cole and Kelly - who else? - combined to see us home 2-0. It was more than just revenge for their win at St. James' in October... it was the Title! And with two games still remaining, we'd done it with time to spare.

Of the last three matches of that momentous season, I had to be content with the one that's been almost forgotten, sandwiched as it was between games that remain to this day at the forefront of the Magpies' recent history. I'd been denied the trip to Grimsby by an exam and was unable to beat the mad scramble for tickets to see Sunday's finale against Leicester at St. James'. So 48 hours after the championship had been clinched, I made my way up to Newcastle to see us play a now meaningless fixture against Oxford. I was reminded of what it felt like to go to that equally overshadowed contest with Luton way back in 1985. It too must lay disregarded, even in the minds of fans that were there. Newcastle went about their business methodically, even if they did look a bit jaded from the celebrations of two nights before. They could be forgiven for that! The result was still a satisfying 2-1 and the 29,500 crowd was rewarded with a stunning turn-on-a-sixpence finish by Coley for our second goal.

The last match has, of course, become folklore on Tyneside and the fact I wasn't there was as much a source of personal regret as missing the last game of the season before. It was sweet irony, nonetheless, that we beat the same club and that this time the reward wasn't just survival, but a first class ticket to The Premier League. Both Andy Cole and Ned Kelly got hat-tricks as Leicester were annihilated 7-1, Newcastle United announcing to the world that we meant business in the new division. Two months later, I followed the Magpies' example and gained 'automatic promotion': BSc (Honours) Applied Biology, Class 2.2. That parallel shift in both our fortunes had happened again!

Fifteen

Fanfare for the Plastic Fan

The underlying principle of being a football fan is not a complex one. Most fans love their club because it's their local team, some because of family tradition and a few, sometimes to a surprising degree of loyalty, simply because they're glory hunters and like backing a winner. Similarly, the idiosyncrasies that go with following a particular team are basically a case of 'follow my leader'. For example, hating Sunderland and, to a lesser degree, Boro goes with the territory when you're a Newcastle fan. You don't necessarily need to have a reason but if you keep the faith long enough you'll inevitably find one.

In my case, despising the Mackems was an essential prerequisite as my career on the terraces at St. James' Park began. I had no personal reason for hating Sunderland, other than a long-lost loathing for my neighbours when I was eight years old. The last time they had inflicted humiliation on Newcastle was in 1979-80, when my major concern was my own playing career at schools and local juniors' club level. I didn't really believe that the Fullwell End was always "full of s***s, full of p***s, and full of w*****s", but I sang along anyway! The play-offs in 1990 changed that view. The sight of the scum celebrating their 2-0 triumph at St. James' etched an indelible image on my memory and was a crime I could never forgive. I really

Fanfare for the Plastic Fan

hated them after that! Likewise, I never had a genuine problem with Middlesbrough. Fans of 'the Boro' were just laughable 'smoggies' - until they tried to lynch and then coin us at Ayresome Park in 1989.

Most fans from this era will tell a largely similar story, either simpler or more elaborate depending on how committed to Newcastle United they were. With few exceptions we all shared other nuances like a favourite other team (Celtic/Rangers or Berwick Rangers), sympathies and hatred of particularly crap referees and ex-Mackem opponents. In the years up to 1992, apart from the full-on hooligans, that's how we all were, just like fans in the '50s wore bobble hats and carried rattles and bells.

A combination of factors contributed to the gradual dilution of this traditional culture at St. James' Park. The marked reduction in football hooliganism and the surge in popularity of football following Italia 90 had led to rising gates at football grounds everywhere. But it was Newcastle's stunning season in 1992-93 that provided the catalyst for a completely new species at St. James' Park. The glory hunter could never have looked at Newcastle United with any sort of desire before that sublime Division One Championship. Since time immemorial, successive teams in the famous black and white had been at best inconsistent, irrespective of what division they were in. The Magpie Group had predicted that this would happen if the problems on the pitch were put right and no one who ever uttered the words "Sack the board" would ever say that they didn't long for the day St. James' Park would be sold out every week. The problem was that factors over and above Newcastle's success were also summoning those hitherto uninterested in football onto the bandwagon. The numbers wanting to buy into the glitzy Premiership future of Newcastle were far greater than the new regime at St. James' Park could ever have expected. The capacity of the ground, once the redevelopments were complete, would still only be 36,000. But now those improvements were making the Gallowgate stadium even more attractive to people who would never have dreamt of enduring the sort of conditions that existed pre-1993.

There would have been nothing wrong with all the new blood at St. James' Park, so long as it hadn't been allowed to usurp the folk who were the lifeblood of the club before 92-93. People who had been going to home matches on a regular basis for years now found the right to take their place in the new ground under threat. The fact that the new administration did nothing to prevent thousands of old supporters having their places taken by wealthier bandwagon jumpers, many of whom had never been to St. James' before that championship season, was a disgrace. I had friends who suffered this cruel indignity. Andy, who had been watching the Toon regularly since 1988, was one. Another was his mate Kenny, who went to every home game in 91-92. It was an early indication of the indifference towards the average fan held in certain quarters of the boardroom.

The new fans were, by and large, uninterested in silly things like singing. They sat quietly, passed around flasks of tea and munched on prawn sandwiches. Nothing wrong with that - there'd been a sizeable contingent for years that used to sit in the old West and then Milburn Stands. Only they'd always gone to matches, even when the football was dire. They were part of the fabric of how things used to be at St. James' Park. Now the new generation of fans seemed to be snubbing their noses at their traditional counterparts. As if to justify the legitimacy of their new order, links were made in certain quarters between the disappearance of the old guard and the reduction in the incidence of hooliganism and racist chanting.

Fanfare for the Plastic Fan

Certainly, the incidence of swearing did go down noticeably, but that was more due to the fact that these new supporters liked to sit quietly and watch, rather than indulge in banter with opposition players and fans. It was as though the new fans were saying, 'We're the future of this football club and it's a cleaner, more sophisticated one. Now you ruffians can be on your way!'

The fault didn't really lie with all new fans who came along in 1992 and 93, an anathema though they were to the more traditional supporter. After all, they were invited in by an administration keen to see the colour of their money, up front and before the start of each season. What should have been done was that a section of the ground be set aside for fans that could only afford to pay on a match-to-match basis. The old Gallowgate End at first, and then a proportion of the seats in the stand that replaced it. It would've been easy to implement and easier still to regulate. But the new board, for all it had done to wrench the club into the modern world, seemed to have lost touch with the very people it had initially sought to represent. After all, had those many thousands of supporters usurped in 1993 not gone along to St. James' Park in 1989, 91 and 92, or even before that in the early eighties, there would have been no Newcastle United for anyone to watch! It was a crying shame the way such loyalty was ignored and an insult to those who were forced out. In a lot of ways, supporting Newcastle United was never the same after 1992-93.

Sixteen

The Final Chapter?

As the dust settled on Newcastle's best league season for almost thirty years, changes were already afoot within St. James' Park. Departures were never going to reach the epidemic proportions they had following United's last promotion in 1984. Nevertheless, it was with shock and some dismay that fans confronted the news that both Ned Kelly and Gavin Peacock were leaving the club. They would both be sorely missed, although their departures were now of little real significance to a squad already oozing Premiership quality.

Keegan himself, of course, was going nowhere. He'd weaved his magic a second time for Newcastle United and, far from the rookie he'd been when he walked through the door eighteen months earlier, KK was now the hottest property in English coaching. And the Magpies were anything but relegation fodder, unlike the grim predictions back in '84. This time, most pundits forecast a trouble-free debut in the top flight - mid-table, at worst. Some of us were even more optimistic, especially when Keegan made the transfer swoop of the summer in ending Peter Beardsley's six-year exile on Merseyside. I genuinely believed we were capable of emulating Blackburn Rovers' feat of finishing fourth in their first Premier League campaign. After all, the top flight was as open as it had been since the early Seventies. The top guns were now less well established, making football's brand new superleague

The Final Chapter?

highly competitive. Alex Ferguson's ageing Manchester United side had lifted the inaugural Premiership crown and teams like Aston Villa, Leeds and Blackburn were expected to be the main pretenders for their first defence.

Like the club I hoped we'd emulate, Newcastle too possessed the distinct advantage of having a rich chairman who wasn't slow in opening his chequebook. Unlike Jack Walker's Blackburn, however, John Hall wasn't intent on building a castle in the sand. Despite unlimited cash for signings, promotion to the Premiership and that impressive first season in it, the Lancashire steel magnate's club had been unable to attract regular gates of much more than 20,000. They'd resorted to doling out free tickets by the thousand to local schoolchildren so their attendances had an air of respectability - they could afford to. Newcastle United, by contrast, was a sleeping giant and Hall, by now Sir John, knew that in the long run he would get back the money he was investing through the gates and the rapidly growing merchandising operation being eagerly gobbled up by the club's massive fan base.

The main problem Newcastle faced now was that this fan base massively exceeded the ground capacity. The revamped stadium (the new stand at the Leazes End was now complete and had quickly been renamed The Sir John Hall Stand) held little more than it had before the redevelopment, as it gradually went all-seater in accordance with new guidelines. In its wisdom, the board decided to make the whole seated area of St. James' Park available only by the purchase of season tickets, with all the new places allocated on a first come first served basis. Needless to say, the whole lot were gone within a few hours of going on sale, leaving a waiting list of tens of thousands who'd been unsuccessful.

Standing in the Corner

There was still space left in St. James' Park, of course - the standing areas, comprising the West Stand Paddock and Gallowgate End. For the first half of 1993-94, the Gallowgate - awaiting demolition - would remain open, with away fans moved from the Leazes End to The Corner. In addition, much-needed overspill for The Toon Army would be provided in The Scoreboard and erstwhile 'Floodlight' sections. Initial sounds suggested that the club would ticket these areas on a match-to-match basis but the stampede for season tickets all over the rest of the ground soon put a stop to that idea. Seeing still more pound signs flashing before their eyes, the club rode back. The standing accommodation too would be available only by a single one-off payment.

I was guilty, as is often the case, of taking my eyes off the game. For the most part, I'd spent the summer driving between Sheffield and Morpeth, preparing to return north to find a job. I couldn't afford a season ticket for the new stand at that stage and was content just to stand on the Gallowgate. I would apply for a ticket in the new stand at that end in twelve months' time. My plan, I believed, was foolproof; after all, I'd thwarted all those bandwagon jumpers for all but the last game of 92-93. However, it was that last game that should have been my wake-up call. I was in Sheffield when the part-season-tickets for the Gallowgate were sold and knew nothing until I phoned the ticket office for information about the opening game against Spurs.

"There are no tickets for Tottenham, the terraced areas are all season ticket now," explained a voice on the other end of the phone.

"So how do I apply for one?" I asked urgently.

"You can't. They were all sold yesterday!"

So that was it then, I'd been usurped. I bet someone not even 'into' football twelve months before had taken my place! Well, I suppose they couldn't possibly have

The Final Chapter?

been expected to go when there were all those nasty hooligans running around everywhere. I imagine they'd have been 'upset' by the rowdy "Sack The Board" protests and 'outraged' by the antics of some of our more demonstrative fans in the olden days. What the f*** would they have made of Crazy Firestarter Raj at Leicester in 1986? Where were THEY when we were s***?

I was contemplating how to go about ending it all when the phone rang. It was Oges. "Did you get one of those part-season-tickets for the Gallowgate?"

"??+*! !¦?? ????!"

"Mm! I thought you might not have heard! Don't worry, I got one and I don't need it now. You can have mine."

It turned out that his uncle had been an engineer working on the construction of the Sir John Hall Stand. He'd been able to reserve a seat for his fanatical nephew. Oges' ticket for the Gallowgate was now surplus to requirement. My old mate had done it again! Twice I'd been effectively banished from getting to see Newcastle and twice Oges had stepped-in at the last minute and bailed me out.

So when that first match of 93-94 arrived on 14th August, it was with some relief, and a far greater air of excitement than I could remember in a long time. Whilst the half-season-ticket I'd fortuitously obtained got me into only the first ten matches, at least I wasn't going to be completely locked out, unlike thousands of other unlucky souls. Some that I knew had to wait years to get back in. Tottenham were by now in decline, following the controversial dismissal of Terry Venables towards the end of the previous season. What's more, unbelievably, they were now being managed by the man who had almost got us relegated to Division Three - Ossie Ardiles - although to Spurs fans, he was still very much a hero. A very expectant

Standing in the Corner

35,000 was in party mood and the rapidly developing ground, now three-quarters complete, made for an impressive backdrop. Even with the Gallowgate still uncovered, St. James' Park already looked better than the homes of many other top flight football clubs. What a difference to the dilapidated stadium of only a few years before!

Somehow, though, the atmosphere just wasn't quite the same. You could cut the tension with a knife, for sure, but a certain something was lacking compared to before. A giant flag, unfurled for the first time on the last day of the promotion season, could now go all the way round from the East Stand to West via the inhabitants of the lower tier of the Sir John Hall Stand. But not even this spectacle, or the sight of dancing girls on the pitch, could compensate for what was missing. My mind went back to previous great occasions in the noble arena, like Keegan's debut in 1982 and the first game back in Division One two years later. Now, whilst there was still that buzz of excitement, just like all those years before, few people bothered to clamber up onto the crush barriers and crowd surges were looked upon as an abomination! It was like when you go back for the first time to a place you've not visited for years, somewhere that harbours fond memories, only to find emptiness, as the people with whom you shared those reminiscences are long gone. The heart and soul of St. James' Park had been taken out. The traditional lifeblood drained away and was replaced by a wealthier, more genteel clientele unable to create the atmosphere such an occasion demanded.

As was inevitably the case when the *Match of the Day* cameras came to town, the game was a dull affair. Newcastle, lacking the experience of Beardsley due to a freak pre-season facial injury, were simply overawed and Tottenham's workmanlike performance was

The Final Chapter?

enough to steal all three points. Ironically, the only goal was scored from almost the exact same spot as Keegan's famous strike against QPR in '82, Teddy Sheringham stealing away from Kevin Scott to score at the Gallowgate End. The Spurs defence kept Andy Cole quiet all afternoon and the party had been spoilt. Keegan would need to go back to the drawing board for the games to come.

And those upcoming games weren't getting any easier! The following Wednesday night, the Magpies visited Coventry for a game packed with incident, in which Newcastle again walked away empty-handed. Inspired by their new striker Micky Quinn, Coventry won 2-1, with Pavel Srnicek sent off and Quinny skying the resultant penalty! Then, just when we didn't need it, the third game involved a visit to the last place on earth you'd want to try to kickstart your season - Old Trafford! And the reigning champions had opened up with two consecutive wins. It looked like Newcastle, still light in the strikers department, faced an uphill struggle in the theatre of so many shattered dreams in years gone by. A draw would have been a fantastic result - did anyone still have Mirandinha's phone number? But it was a player who was very much a part of Newcastle United's present who ensured the shaky start didn't become a mighty wobble in this most unlikely of settings. Andy Cole was about to show the Premiership exactly why he'd earned such a fearsome reputation in Division One, and there was no better place to start in earnest than at the home of the champions! The Reds had stolen the lead early in the second half, but with ten minutes to go, the Magpies struck back through the industrious Cole. Accepting a return pass from summer signing Nicky Papavasilou, Coley darted into the area to sidefoot past the sprawling Schmeichel. Four days later, United recorded their first Premiership victory, a 1-0 success at home to Everton. But, despite dominating the game, we had to wait until midway through the second half for the winner, arriving when Malcolm Allen, deputising for Beardsley, saw his deflected shot loop over the head of Neville Southall. It had been touch and go but, at last, Newcastle were up and running in the big league.

Successive 1-1 draws followed against Blackburn and Ipswich, with Cole adding to his account in both matches. Then came the game which really saw Newcastle United's arrival on the big stage, a thrilling 4-2 success over Sheffield Wednesday at St. James' Park. In a bizarre twist, both teams were forced to change colours, as Newcastle's traditional black and white stripes clashed with both Wednesday's home and away kits. It led to the hasty introduction of a green 'third' kit, worn intermittently throughout the season, until that too clashed - with the newly introduced colours of Premier League match officials! The Wednesday game really was a firecracker, as the scoreline suggests. The more passive 'new' St. James' Park crowd gave Chris Waddle a far less torrid reception than in his Spurs days, and he, in turn, caused United interminable problems down both flanks before Newcastle managed to step up a gear in the second half. Cole, whose stature was rising by the game, helped himself to two more goals, Allen got one and victory was sealed in spectacular style by a wonder goal from Scots starlet Alex Mathie. No wonder Sky Sports, who were televising the game live, had dubbed us "The Entertainers".

In between the Sheffield Wednesday and Everton victories, I'd actually missed a home game - the 1-1 draw with Blackburn. It was Oges' fault! His efforts to have his wedding arranged in the cricket season had been thwarted by the long-suffering Lesley, so he'd resorted to booking it on a Sunday, the bank holiday

The Final Chapter?

weekend of August 29th. Enter Sky Sports, who seemed to have anticipated Newcastle's Entertainers billing and promptly rearranged the fixture for their live Super Sunday coverage. I was to be best man, so we were both well and truly scuppered, along with the uncle who'd inadvertently saved me from Toon exile and half the sizeable Ogle clan of South East Northumberland. Even the photographer compounded the situation. A perfectionist, he made the whole process take forever and we had to rely on Oges' Uncle Ian, who was scurrying back and forwards from his hotel room, to keep us up to date with the score!

Form remained patchy until mid-October, when finally the return of Peter Beardsley to the side marked an upturn in our performances. Newcastle's next five games saw a draw with Swindon, two 2-0 wins over West Ham and Villa, and 1-2 defeats to QPR and Southampton. The Rangers game, at home on 16th October, gave further indication of the sort of people who were 'taking over' St. James' Park. QPR were an exciting side managed by Gerry Francis and had Sir Les Ferdinand, the Dani Behr-friendly aerial battering ram, as their principle threat. For the first twenty minutes, Ferdinand remained a constant danger as Rangers soaked up all of Newcastle's pressure and hit back on the break time and again. Then Sir Les went down injured and was off the pitch by the dug-out for a lengthy period of treatment.

"Thank God for that!" I remarked, my voice hoarse from chanting, "they're sure to take him off now!"

"That's a pretty poor attitude!" replied a middle-aged gent who was standing next to me, clearly feeling the need to reply to my rhetorical comment. "I've been looking forward to seeing him play all week. That's the sort of attitude I'd expect from someone like you. Have you yobs learnt nothing of what football's about nowadays?"

Standing in the Corner

If I'd made a racist comment, his sentiments would have been spot-on, but I didn't and, I can quite honestly say, never had made any racist comments at any football match. And I'd been to nearly 300 by that time. Moments later, Les was back on the pitch and had given QPR the lead as the Londoners hit us on the break yet again. My point exactly! We hit back, early in the second half, through a magnificent Malcolm Allen volley, but Rangers pinched another goal and then hung on by the skins of their teeth as Allen missed an injury-time penalty.

Beardsley's eventual return coincided with a majestic ascent up the Premier League table from middling to top six. This was largely thanks to a twenty-point haul from the nine games leading up to Christmas. Things were now going well on the pitch, but beneath the surface, unrest was bubbling up in certain quarters. Newcastle had gone out of the League Cup early, yet again; beaten 2-1 in round three by our serial bogey-team Wimbledon. Mysteriously missing from the side was Andy Cole and the reason for his absence was soon to be splashed across the back pages of all the daily newspapers. Coley had gone AWOL on arrival in London following a bust-up with Keegan and McDermott. It was the first instance of the alleged 'attitude' problem that had been highlighted in his time as a youth player at Arsenal, an issue that would resurface at regular intervals throughout his career. On closer analysis, however, Cole's fit of pique may well have been justified on this occasion. A native of Nottingham who had spent his formative years in London, Andy had fallen victim to either poor advice, or a complete lack of it following the completion of his move to Newcastle. Cole had bought his house in the one-horse market town of Crook, in the foothills of the County Durham Pennines. On the face of it, not the sort of place a young professional footballer would find much to interest him, but shouldn't someone at the club have advised him thus? A combination of homesickness and boredom, initially identified in the press as attitude, became a little more understandable once the full story became clear. Meanwhile, Cole's best mate, Lee Clark, had also fallen foul of KK and Terry Mac after he kicked over a bucket of water upon being substituted in the defeat at Southampton. Clarkie was reprimanded for the incident and later issued an unreserved apology. The problems with both players were amicably resolved, but throughout the rest of the season, player trouble at Newcastle was never far from the surface.

The three home games in November were nonetheless marked by inspirational performances from the Magpies. Beardsley grabbed a hat trick on his 'home debut' against Wimbledon, a 4-0 annihilation that went some of the way towards compensating us for their win in the League Cup. Pedro was again in inspired form as Sheffield United fell by the same score on a snowy night towards the end of the month. But it was the 3-0 demolition of Liverpool, at St. James' Park on November 21st, that really pointed to where Newcastle were heading. Cole grabbed all three in almost identical circumstances before the break as he, Beardsley and left-winger Scott Sellars appeared to have developed telepathic communication. How far the Magpies had come in such a short time under Keegan. Liverpool weren't exactly the world-beaters of old, but considering the club's position less than two years earlier, it was a transition of monumental proportions.

And just to up the ante on all the half million Scousers, three weeks later United went to Goodison Park and recorded our first away win over Everton since 1960. "Thank you very much for Peter Beardsley, thank you very much, thank you very-very-very much!" sang the Toon Army from the Gwladys Street

End as Pedro, a Toffees player less than six months before, made it 2-0 with only five minutes left. United were now in the top six and all my crazy dreams were coming true! Apart from a 2-1 reverse at Arsenal, we didn't lose another game until after Christmas, a run that included tricky home games with both Leeds and Man United and the return visit to Spurs. Beardsley once again showed his class at White Hart Lane with a breathtaking individual goal; similar to one he scored there way back in 1986. It was late in the game and with Tottenham having just equalised Newcastle's early lead, Pedro's brilliance stole back the initiative and guaranteed us three more precious points. Another landmark Keegan signing was doing the business for United!

And before 1994 was two months old, Keegan was opening the St. James' Park chequebook again, as seemingly limitless funds were made available to strengthen the team. The name of Darren Peacock, the erstwhile QPR central defender who looked more like he'd just quit Whitesnake, was added to that of Norwich winger Ruel Fox and new squad numbers soared to dizzy heights. The size of the first team pool was now sufficient to give the manager a headache over team selection, not to mention the problems encountered by the fourth official with his substitutes board! The problem I had envisaged - of missing the second half of the season once the demolition of the Gallowgate got under way - was alleviated when the club discovered it could proceed with the project whilst keeping the bottom section of the terrace open. The board announced that by excluding away supporters, they could accommodate all of the standing home support for the whole of 93-94. My half-season-ticket was duly renewed!

Newcastle had started the new year in the same way as we'd rounded off the old, with three straight wins in the league and progress, at the expense of Coventry,

The Final Chapter?

into the fourth round of the FA Cup. With the Magpies now occupying fourth spot in the Premiership, the season was going ahead of expectation, but the next spot of trouble at Newcastle United lay just around the corner. The sticky patch began when Southampton, another Newcastle bogey team of old, came to St. James' Park towards the end of January. Lurking dangerously close to the foot of the table and in nondescript form, they were expected to be easy meat for a black and white outfit now on top of its game. Of course, we had reckoned without their talisman Matt le Tissier, who had single-handedly destroyed us at The Dell in October. United were uncharacteristically poor on a day on which, owing to the lack of away fans, a deathly hush fell over St. James' Park. Southampton were unquestionably the better side, but we were all mightily relieved when Andy Cole equalised in the last minute to seemingly give us an undeserved share of the spoils. Enter le Tissier, whose lethal danger was lost on no one when Southampton won an injury-time free kick close to the edge of our penalty area. We all held our breath as the Channel Islander stepped up... and curled his shot past statuesque Newcastle keeper, Mike Hooper - 2-1. Bastard! He'd done it again. The winning run was in tatters and the Trappist Army filed out of our cathedral to mull over just what had gone wrong.

Seven days later, we were back to witness an equally muted performance both on the pitch and in the stands. This time the opposition was Second Division Luton in the FA Cup, with their manager, the ubiquitous David Pleat, having done his homework on the system he expected the Magpies to employ. Keegan's tactics allowed full-backs Beresford and Watson, both attack-minded, to overlap - frequently resulting in them doubling up as additional wide players. The plan thrived on the fact that when they

Standing in the Corner

weren't defending, both Watto and Bez were in space and available to receive the ball from midfield. Pleat countered this by pushing both his wide midfielders onto our full-backs, denying us the additional outlet that led to a lot of our attacking down the flanks. It was a defensively-minded scheme, but one which resulted in the lower division side leading for much of the game. A late equaliser from the penalty spot by Beardsley saved the Magpies' blushes, but it was only to be an eleven-day stay of execution. In the replay, at Kenilworth Road, Luton repeated the same tactic, hoping to hit us on the break to win the tie without recourse to penalties. It worked, as almost continuous possession for United still failed to break down the Hatters and the home side scored twice on the counter, through emerging striker John Hartson.

So our last realistic chance of silverware that season was gone. And, by the end of the next league game, even the vague hope that the Premiership title still offered would be all but snuffed out. I'd been working in a temporary capacity at a pharmaceuticals company in Northumberland, and was stuck on emergency tax by the agency that had sent me there. Before the next league game, away at Wimbledon, I had a pleasant surprise - a cheque for four hundred quid landed on my doormat, the tax rebate I was owed. Get in! I decided to blow a portion of it on an away game and so two days later, I was on my way to South London, hoping for a major upturn in our fortunes.

My dilapidated Nissan Micra wasn't up to the long journey. It was essential for getting me to work anyway, so I decided to resort to old-fashioned means of transport - Intercity - to get me down to London and back. The irony was that the effort I was making should, at the very least, have rewarded me with a new league ground. Unfortunately, Wimbledon were now

The Final Chapter?

groundsharing with Crystal Palace, so for me this was only a repeat visit to Selhurst Park. Paradoxically, although I'd now been here twice, I'd never seen Newcastle play the Eagles, as my previous excursion with Raj back in 1986 had been when Charlton were their lodgers!

It was a bizarre setting for a Premiership match. The only game Newcastle played in all season that wasn't all-ticket, the gate of 13,358 was more than half made up by the travelling arm of the Toon Army. That didn't bother the Dons of course, they were used to it, and they showed little mercy as they tore into their out-of-sorts opponents. Albeit by a more aerial route, Wimbledon were even more commanding than we'd been in beating them 4-0 in the corresponding fixture, and from the terraces all we could do was try our best to lift our side, using our numerical advantage. But the best we could muster in the first half was the cruel "You couldn't score with your brother!" directed at John Fashanu as he missed as hatful of chances! The generosity in front of goal didn't last long though, as Fash and co soon discovered their shooting boots and raced into a two-goal lead before the break. Even a fortuitous penalty, converted by Beardsley immediately on half-time, couldn't stem the tide. After the interval, the home side continued to take the initiative, the air traffic on final approach to Gatwick taking a considerable battering! Two more goals made it 4-1 and if they'd taken all their chances, it might well have been seven or eight. Another late Pedro penalty meant at least the final score had some degree of respectability, but it had been another day of misery for the travelling black and white hordes.

On the way home, apart from having to endure a booze ban, courtesy of Boro fans getting on at Peterborough, the journey became even more sombre when it emerged that yet another player crisis had erupted within the club. It was revealed that several players, led by supposed senior pro Barry Venison, had broken curfew during the three-day interval between the Luton and Wimbledon games, and gone on the razzle in London! Keegan had shown he could be forgiving with regard to younger players, but this spelt the effective end of Venison at Newcastle. He lasted out the rest of the season, but incoming transfers thereafter saw him quickly edged out of the picture at St. James' Park. Mike Hooper, too, was a casualty of the Wimbledon catastrophe, although he was in no way involved in the curfew-busting. Many fans seemed to hold him solely responsible for the downturn in our fortunes and, not for the first time, sections within the Toon Army ranks turned on an individual player as the fall guy for the failings of the whole team. Whilst Hooper had put in a mistake-ridden display at Selhurst Park, he'd also pulled off several outstanding saves and it wasn't surprising to discover that many of his fiercest critics hadn't even been to Wimbledon. Nevertheless, Hooper's bloopers cost him his place in the side and the passing of the goalkeeper's jersey to Pavel Srnicek saw an eventual upturn in our fortunes.

No one doubted the class in the squad Keegan had assembled, so the poor run of form had to end sooner or later. When it did, a run of six consecutive victories coincided with the arrival of spring and Newcastle United's ascent back up the table was marked by some impressive performances. First, Coventry were battered 4-0 as St. James' Park at last rediscovered its voice. A somewhat fortuitous victory at Sheffield Wednesday followed, the opportunity for me to revisit my most recent stamping ground highlighted by a boozy post-match celebration. The 'West Street Wobble' certainly lived up to its name that evening! Next on the list was Swindon, play-off winners in 92-

The Final Chapter?

93 but way out of their depth in the top flight and marooned ten points adrift at the bottom of the pile. The Magpies showed no mercy as John Gorman's side were annihilated 7-1, and our goal difference was boosted still further with comfortable wins over West Ham, Ipswich and Norwich.

Another three-match winless sequence followed, but that too was ended in emphatic style with a 2-0 victory over Liverpool at Anfield. "Thank you very much for the twelve points, Scousers!" sang the Toon Army, paraphrasing our efforts at Goodison just before Christmas! Well, we had to make the most of it - surely Liverpool would never be so generous again. So far, ten years on, they never have! Then, following a 3-2 home win over doomed Oldham Athletic, came arguably the pick of the bunch. On a glorious April evening, Aston Villa, the previous season's runners-up in the league, were blown away 5-1, with Newcastle at times mesmerising. The absence of Paul McGrath from the Villa line-up, for undisclosed reasons, did nothing to diminish United's top-drawer performance, and he wouldn't have been able to do anything, anyway, to prevent a spectacular thirty-yard strike from Paul Bracewell setting us on our way. But it gave the Toon Army the opportunity to ask, "Where's your boozy centre half?" of Villa boss Ron Atkinson, on an evening that still stands out as one of the finest in the recent past of Newcastle United. And another landmark was set. Andy Cole, who along with Beardsley had been in blistering form all season, became the first ever Magpies player to reach 40 goals in a season. The previous best, George Robledo's 39 in 1951-52, had come in a more free-scoring era of the game, making Coley's feat all the more outstanding! Newcastle, at last, had a genuine successor to those grand custodians of the famous old number nine shirt.

Standing in the Corner

Even a 0-2 reverse at Bramall Lane on the second last Saturday of the season wasn't enough to dent the Magpies' by now cast-iron UEFA Cup credentials. The significance of our final game of the season, at home to Arsenal, became meaningless when the Gooners won the Cup Winners' Cup in midweek, making either third or fourth place sufficient to qualify for Europe's third major competition. In the end, it mattered not as we defeated George Graham's charges 2-0 to cement third position in the Premiership. It had been a magnificent first season back in the big league, better than anything since way back in the Fifties. It seemed a long time since we had so narrowly avoided relegation to Division Three. It was, in fact, only two years, but so much had changed at Newcastle United. That change was also about to include the last part of the ground I still recognised. I'd been able to spend the last four months of the season standing in The Corner, the place I'd learned my trade as a Toon Army foot soldier. A fortnight later it would all be gone, replaced by August with an all-seater stand - my new home. As we filed out of the old terrace for the last time, the bulldozers were already poised, having all but demolished the top section already. It was a poignant reminder of what life used to be like at St. James' Park. Now Newcastle United was a very different club, forward-thinking and ambitious. What sort of future lay ahead for us when we returned in four months to our newly-completed stadium?

Seventeen

European Dreams

The summer of 1994 was one of the best I can remember. It might have had something to do with the pride I felt at Newcastle United's inspirational first season in the Premiership. It might have been because of a brief liaison with a girl who didn't seem to care how much football I watched, beer I drank or even how often I sloped off fishing. That was until she suddenly dumped me for a teetotal vegan with an aversion to the beautiful game! Still, there were plenty more fish in the sea - or the river Swale, to be exact - and in any case, it was the first week of USA 94, four weeks of non-stop footy!

I actually enjoyed this World Cup. Strange as it may seem, it was probably because England had failed to qualify, making the whole tournament seem less stressful. No reason to worry about their slow start, probable failure to get past the quarter-finals and the ominous form of Italy, Germany and Argentina, the only three countries to have won the competition in the last quarter of a century. Ironically, the big guns all started slowly, leaving the early limelight to be grabbed by smaller nations like Belgium and Switzerland, both entertaining sides, if at times a little cavalier in their approach to the game. They went into every match looking simply to out-score the opposition and Kevin Keegan, working as a TV pundit, was clearly impressed judging by his pre-season transfer activity following the month-long spectacle. In the end, it was everyone's other second favourite team that emerged as the winners. Brazil got their hands back on the trophy for the first time since Newcastle United were Fairs Cup holders, with toothy teenage sensation Ronaldo racing onto the pitch brandishing a flag following their victory over Italy on penalties.

England may have failed to book their place at the big event in the US, but I wasn't about to do likewise and miss out on my right to a seat in the new stand being built on the Gallowgate End. It was due to be complete for the start of 1994-95 and I had a cunning plan and £300 of my tax rebate still burning a hole in my pocket to make sure I got my way. During the close season, the club had made great play of the fact that they had put their money where their mouth was in securing both Andy Cole, and Kevin Keegan himself, on ten-year contracts. A leafleting campaign that coincided with season ticket renewals urged fans to do likewise and promised that if we could cough up the princely sum of a monkey, the club would swing it for us to retain our seats for a whole decade. The bold promises were not the issue to me - indeed, in the case of the Save Our Seats campaigners less than five years later, the guarantees seemed a little hollow. What I was actually well aware of was that if I bought one of these so-called 'bonds', I could ensure I jumped the queue in the waiting list. The trials and tribulations of twelve months before had taught me a valuable lesson - I should look after number one and not let ten years of loyal support in the lean years be appropriated by two years of glory-hunting.

So I paid the five hundred notes and a few weeks later received the news I had been so eagerly expecting - confirmation that I'd been allocated a seat in the new stand for the coming season. The bond conferred other benefits too - free home cup matches for three years, which as Newcastle had qualified for the UEFA Cup, was a significant bonus. But the single most important detail to me was that I had secured my place at St. James' Park and if I were put in that position again I would definitely do the same thing.

There were certainly voices of discontent at the way the club had acted in the characteristic way that the chattering classes muse over issues they contend. There was also criticism of the 'unsporting' way that fans like me had unfairly queue 'jumped' by buying a bond. Where were those voices twelve months earlier during the initial mad scramble for season tickets, when many of these principled folk were using their financial advantage to usurp less wealthy fans? I'm sure most could probably have afforded five hundred quid, but believed the cost too extortionate for a game of football. But what price do you place on something that has become a part of your life? I felt no reason to sense guilt for what I had done. My moral high ground was that I had been there when things were crap and had every right to enjoy the good times as well.

Other close season business was less contentious. Keegan, seemingly now secure in his position for as long as he wanted, soon set about investing some more of the club's earnings on further strengthening the squad. KK's reconnaissance during the World Cup proved fruitful as he sought to add strength and flair to the Magpies' backline. Central defender Philippe Albert and right-back Marc Hottiger, both stars of the Mundial who had played for Belgium and Switzerland respectively, were inserted into the squad at a combined cost of £5 million. Paul Kitson, a centre forward from Derby, soon followed for £2.25 million to provide back-up for the hard-working Beardsley and Cole. With Keegan's first season of consolidation in the Premiership having delivered qualification for Europe, Newcastle now possessed a side looking well capable of the manager's much heralded four-pronged campaign for silverware.

Once again the title race was expected to be open. Manchester United had retained their Premiership crown in 93-94, with Kenny Dalglish's Blackburn, who were even bigger spenders than us, their principal rivals. Liverpool, having replaced Graeme Souness with club stalwart Roy Evans, would surely be contenders and apart from them, the usual suspects lurked in the wings, most notably Leeds and Arsenal. It was billed as the most exciting season ever, with the traditional big guns all back to full strength and the new guns, us and Blackburn, equally likely to mount a challenge. And with the magnificent new St. James' Park now all but complete, the stage was set for Newcastle United's first genuine league championship quest for almost half a century.

I had deliberately stayed away from St. James' over the summer months. I wanted to maximise the impact of my first sight of the new Gallowgate End, branded the Exhibition Stand in my new season ticket book. And I wasn't disappointed. In place of the old brick turnstiles was a monumental structure with steel piles and stanchions disappearing into the sky above Strawberry Place. It was far grander than the stand built the previous year at the Leazes End as it soared high above the surrounding land to compensate for the steep bank that had been removed during construction. Entry was via a staircase made up of robust scaffolding, as the eventual paved steps were to be built at the same time as the corners were filled in later in the season. For the time being, our new kop was a freestanding structure separated from the rest of the ground by a small gap on either side. The turnstiles were situated on a concrete boulevard suspended above the main road below, allowing the police to keep Strawberry Place open to through-traffic on matchdays

European Dreams

for the first time in fifty years. Turnstile 58 opened into a cavernous foyer, with bars and bookmakers lining its seventy-yard expanse. This catered for supporters, who, like me, were housed in the lower and middle tiers of the new stand. High above, near the top of the structure, was a near-identical amenity for fans living in the upper tier. Its glass front afforded a spectacular view down to the river Tyne and over Gateshead and beyond. Climbing the small flight of steps leading out of the foyer immediately opposite the turnstiles brought you up into the main seated area. It was like going down the tunnel onto the pitch. One second you were in a bar area and the next you were inside the magnificent St. James' Park amphitheatre. My seat was fantastic as well. I seemed to be hovering slightly above crossbar level, just outside the right hand goalpost, such was the pitch of the new stand compared with the terracing it had replaced. I didn't know any of my neighbours but I wasn't going to have to wait long to find out what they were like, as Newcastle proceeded to lay on a performance out of the top drawer against a stunned Coventry City.

The 4-0 demolition of the Sky Blues was the second game of an inspirational start to the season by the Magpies, newly-promoted Leicester having already succumbed 3-1 at Filbert Street. The third game saw Southampton visit St. James' Park and become the second team in four days to lose by a four-goal margin. Watson, Cole and Lee shared the goals for the second game in a row as the Saints endured martyrdom to the tune of 5-1 in the new coliseum on Barrack Road. Such magnificent performances and the now completely enclosed stadium led to the sort of carnival atmosphere that had only rarely been seen in the previous campaign, in spite of the eventual top-three finish. New songs began to be heard for the first time in ages, the best of all the classic, 'Philippe, Philippe

Standing in the Corner

Albert, everyone knows his name'. I soon discovered that the bloke next to me talked a very good game. He was constantly commenting throughout the match, although, except for the occasional "United", he hardly ever raised his voice. He had his own personalised ditty for each player, particularly the impressive new signings: "Hot..." whenever Marc Hottiger was on the ball and "Feed the bear..." for Albert, paraphrasing Roy Aitken's rallying call from the dark days of the early nineties. His advice to any opposition player already booked who was disputing a refereeing decision was simple: "Keep talking!"

The way Newcastle were playing there was no need for any sort of dissent from the stands in the opening two months of the season. Next on the list for annihilation were West Ham, beaten 3-1 at Upton Park, and then Chelsea, hammered 4-2 in front of the *Match of the Day* cameras at St. James'. Coley hit a contender for goal of the season, beating Karhime at his near post with a shot of ferocious power, and the Blues' poison dwarf Dennis Wise, always a crowd favourite at Newcastle, was dismissed on the hour to round off a perfect afternoon. Eight days later came the first championship six-pointer and the Toon's start to the season scaled still greater heights with a 3-2 win over Arsenal at Highbury. Six straight wins and a points gap already starting to open between United and the chasing pack, it seemed that nothing could stop us.

Unfortunately the something that did was Liverpool and their prolific marksman Ian Rush, but even so we should still have taken three more points and recorded a seventh straight win. Newcastle had led 1-0 for much of the game through a strike by Lee, but things took an unexpected twist when Albert was sent off for a second booking midway through the second half. The extra man gave Liverpool renewed hope of getting something

European Dreams

out of a game in which they had been clearly second best. Even then, it took a monumental howler by Pavel Srnicek to gift the Reds a share of the points. Rush was starting to drift through the middle more freely in the absence of Albert and was inevitably going to cause the home defence problems. After peppering the advertising hoardings, the Welshman eventually managed to get a shot on target, but when he did, it was a tame strike aimed straight at the goalkeeper. Sadly for the Toon Army, preparing to celebrate another win in a title six-pointer, Pav took his eye off the ball at the last second and it bobbled straight through him and into the net. Liverpool were happy to hold on to what they had and the game fizzled out into a 1-1 draw. Newcastle had dropped their first points of the season.

Meanwhile, United's UEFA Cup crusade had begun in the same spectacular fashion as the blockbuster Premiership campaign. Our first round opponents, on paper, looked the sort of strong opposition we should have expected to face, having not featured in Europe for seventeen years. Whilst Keegan's men had been fighting their way to promotion in 1992-93, Royal Antwerp had gone all the way to the final of the Cup Winners' Cup, only losing out at the last hurdle to Italian giants Parma. They had qualified for Europe in six out of the last seven seasons. Yet, as we would find with Bayer Leverkusen in the Champion's League eight years later, Antwerp's success had spelt decimation for their exciting young side, the best players targeted ruthlessly by more fashionable clubs. The eleven which lined up against the Magpies was a shadow of the team that had played at Wembley less than eighteen months before and, away from home, United romped into a 5-0 first leg advantage. It was the performance of Robert Lee's career as he helped himself to a hat-trick - all headers - and Keegan was as euphoric as the pocket of

Standing in the Corner

travelling Newcastle fans that braved the crumbling Bosuil Stadium. He praised his midfield genius to the skies, saying Lee's performance proved beyond doubt he was good enough to play for England. Rob would fulfil his manager's prophecy before the following month was out and Newcastle had paralleled the achievements of their 1969 forebears, sweeping aside supposedly higher-ranked opponents and making the return a formality.

The unbeaten run was further stretched to ten games with a customary 2-0 win at Villa Park and a seven-goal thriller in the second leg against Antwerp - the 5-2 success all the more memorable for the fact it was my first ever European match. The UEFA Cup fate of our next opponents couldn't have been more different. Blackburn had just been embarrassingly knocked out of the competition in their first ever tie by Swedish minnows Trelleborgs. The whole episode had left the BBC with almost as much egg on their faces as Rovers, as they had ignored our 10-2 triumph and elected instead to screen both legs of the Lancashire club's 2-3 aggregate defeat! But whilst Blackburn's European record was undistinguished, they were about to show that, at Premiership level, they had still a lot they could teach us, even on our own patch. Only a rather fortunate late equaliser preserved our invincibility this time, as another two points went begging at home against championship rivals. It was a sobering reminder that the glamorous UEFA nights cut no ice on the unforgiving battlefield of domestic football. A lot of the early momentum was starting to be lost as, one by one, the top sides took the fizz out of our lightning start.

For the time being, though, the rich vein of form continued. There were three more consecutive victories, two in the league against Crystal Palace and Sheffield Wednesday, and a third in the UEFA Cup

European Dreams

Second Round first leg at home to Athletic Bilbao. On the surface everything seemed to be progressing as it had from day one, but it was to be that third crunch European game that proved to be the watershed in 94-95, one from which Newcastle United would never fully recover.

The scene on that crisp October evening was that of a classic midweek European cup tie. The sparkling new St. James' Park glistened under the floodlights and an expectant 32,000 crowd soaked up the atmosphere, warming to this new spectacle denied for so long under the austere regime of old. Some of my fondest childhood memories had been watching midweek games on *Sportsnight*. It was pure theatre played out on luminescent floodlit football pitches, the drama somehow heightened by black and white television. The following night would invariably see me out kicking a ball around under some streetlight with friends, trying to re-enact the events. By the time I'd become a regular on the terraces, midweek games always seemed more fun, probably as much because of the new delights of the pub or club after the game. This was the period of near-English dominance just before the Heysel ban, when clubs like Villa, Liverpool, Spurs and Everton seemed to be winning just about every European trophy on offer. I watched their seemingly endless cup runs on TV in both awe and jealousy, wishing we could see a return to nights of European glory at St. James' Park. Back then, of course, it could never have happened, even without the consequences of Heysel. But now, with our football club very much on the up, we were at last seeing the dividend of all the hard work that had been done by Sir John Hall and Keegan in the past few years. Newcastle United, top of the Premiership, were the great black and white hope of English football. The TV cameras had come to town and we would be appearing on nearly every TV set in the country. It was time to put on a really big performance.

For the first hour and ten minutes, the unstoppable Magpies proceeded to do exactly that. United were irresistible, tearing into the Basque side, who were barely able to get a foot on the ball. Goals had to come! After only ten minutes Ruel Fox fired us into a 1-0 lead and before half-time Beardsley made it two from the penalty spot after a foul on Cole. By the hour mark it was 3-0 as a right wing cross from the irrepressible Fox found Coley unmarked to head home his thirteenth goal of the season. It looked destined to be a rout and the atmosphere was as charged as I could remember. But in the final quarter our inexperience at this level began to show, and for the first time that season Newcastle's defence began to look far from watertight! Instead of shutting up shop, we continued to press forward, almost as if it was a one-off cup-tie with no second leg. It was a high risk, zero caution strategy, for which the name of Newcastle United was about to become infamous. Bilbao needed a break and that is exactly what they proceeded to get! First, Ciganda capitalised on a defensive error to reduce Bilbao's arrears to two. Then substitute Suances popped up to make it 3-2, a far less dominant scoreline to take to the north coast of Spain. A double chance spurned by Albert could have sent us into the second leg with more margin for error, but it had been a case of game over and then game back on in the space of just 20 second-half minutes for United.

In truth, we never recovered anything like the early season form after that. Bold statements of intent from Cole, Albert and Keegan hid the reality, at least for another ten days. After all, we were still unbeaten and another win was added to the sequence before things really did start to go pear-shaped - a 2-0 home win over Manchester United's reserves in the League Cup. At least we were definitely through to the next round in that competition! But the Red Devils were only saving their big guns for what they regarded as the more important fixture. Three days later, on 29th October at Old Trafford, it was high noon for our seventeen-match unblemished record. Alex Ferguson was playing catch-up and this time he did mean business. Two second-half goals put paid to that proud unbeaten run as the Cockney Reds gained precise revenge for their defeat three days before. Nonetheless, it had been by far our best start to a season since time immemorial. Even in the promotion charge of two years before, we had already lost twice as many games by this stage. It showed just how far Keegan had brought Newcastle, even since then - the best playing season anyone under the age of thirty could recall!

But what was about to happen next would show us just how far we still had to go if we were to achieve complete success at this level. Three days later a 0-1 scoreline in Bilbao confirmed all our worst fears. Those two late away goals had, after all, cost us our place in the UEFA Cup third round. Only a week before we had been celebrating seventeen games unbeaten, now we had lost twice in not so many more days. We were out of one competition prematurely and our lead at the top of the Premiership had been slashed to just two points, with Liverpool and Blackburn both to play away. It was a return to the harsh realities of top level football after three months of Utopian dreams.

By the end of the week, we were at least back to winning ways in the league, albeit in less than convincing fashion, with a 2-1 home win over QPR. In typical style, all the main contenders won also, meaning we were unable to extend our lead and the unnerving feeling of Man United, Blackburn and Liverpool all breathing down our necks became almost unbearable. It's strange how great a two-point margin seems when you're trying to catch up, yet how slender it feels when you're the side out in front. As I tuned the radio in after the game, waiting at the queue for the lights on Percy Street, Radio Five's football correspondent was berating Newcastle for our loss of form, whilst praising our major rivals to the skies for their ability to 'grind out results' against the run of play. "Typical f***ing BBC!" I muttered as the traffic moved away. The Blackburn UEFA Cup issue had been characteristic of their institutionalised bias towards football clubs in the North West and London and they had been dying to lay into us as soon as our run of form came to an end. But on this occasion, the w***er on the radio had a point, however insincere his motive. We really weren't the side that had started the season so convincingly and the writing had been on the wall long before the defeats at Manchester United and Bilbao.

In the weeks following the Old Trafford loss, our league form became increasingly patchy. A creditable 0-0 draw at surprise title contenders Forest was followed by another miserable defeat at route one bastards Wimbledon. The L column on the back page of the *Pink* became 3 two weeks later at Spurs, and in the home match that divided the two doses of capital punishment, the Toon Army endured the torture of a 1-1 draw at home to bottom side Ipswich. It was inexplicable. What had happened to the side that had murdered Royal Antwerp 5-0 away only nine weeks before? There is no doubt that any side can go off the boil, but when the loss of form coincides with injuries, the effect can be multiplied by several orders of magnitude. Often the indispensable players can be the ones you least expect. In our case, the loss of Scott Sellars, out for the rest of the season, did irrevocable damage to a side whose fluency depended on quick-thinking Salty's ability to receive the ball and pass without a second's thought. Our play suddenly became laboured in his absence, Beardsley's incisive passing game, in particular, hampered by the absence of its most frequent outlet.

And, predictably, as the supply dried up so did the return from our goalscoring ace, Andy Cole. It had long been an open secret that our erstwhile net-buster had been suffering from the painful ailment of shin splints. The open whisper on Tyneside was, to aid his recovery, Cole would need a lengthy spell on the sidelines at some stage in the season. That was the reason Keegan had invested those millions on Paul Kitson. We all envisaged Kitson's time to lead the Newcastle United line would come sooner or later, but no-one could ever have predicted the circumstances that would eventually bring it about.

Our form continued to nosedive in the run-up to Christmas. A 3-1 win over Leicester the week after the Spurs reverse did little to convince the doubters. The Foxes, just promoted, were already well on their way to making a quick return to the First Division. Albert chipped in with two goals, the last of his brief but inspirational entrance onto the St. James' Park stage. He soon became the next name on the list of long-term injuries - cruciate ligament damage ruling him out, like Sellars, for the rest of the campaign. As the festive season gathered momentum, things just got worse. Four days before Christmas, we were knocked out of a second cup competition, losing 0-2 at home to Manchester City in a League Cup fourth round replay. We were starting to look a very ordinary side, struggling to find any semblance of form. A cheerworthy 0-0 draw at Leeds on Boxing Day was followed by a dreadful 1-2 reverse at Norwich three days later. The result may have ensured that the Canaries maintained a respectable mid-table position for now. But they were destined to endure a winless sequence from that game onwards that would see them abseil down the Premiership table and plunge headlong into Division One. Man United or Blackburn would have eaten them for breakfast. On New Year's Day, the misery was complete. Once again, we failed to score at home to Alan Ball's struggling Man City, the only consolation being that this time we managed not to concede. However, the one thing we did all have to concede as we filed out of a depressed St. James' Park was the Premiership title. Barring some kind of miracle, that was now bound for Old Trafford or Blackburn. Our poor run had left us trailing in third place and there was no way that we had any chance of catching back up.

By now, of course, there had been a sea-change in the atmosphere around our brand new super-stadium! The downturn in our fortunes had come as a shock - the way we had begun the season showed little sign that the whole thing would blow up even before Christmas. It had become easy to be complacent - even those of us who should have known better fell into the trap. The real bad times now felt a lifetime away, even though it was actually less than three years. Form had become something we took for granted; after all, last season Newcastle United hadn't suffered anything worse than a wobble, and the year before that, nothing more serious than a blip! Now, the one thing that had kept the splintering Toon Army factions as one - that fantastic start - had dissolved into a nightmare and all kinds of different people had all manner of different solutions to the problem. Many, mainly newcomers used only to winning, just kept quiet, giving rise at times to an eerie silence that somehow echoed around the concrete amphitheatre as if it was empty. Others, in the time-honoured tradition that in 1990 had earned a section of the crowd *The Mag's* headline "Good Moaning, West

European Dreams

Stand!" berated the players and hurled abuse even in Keegan's direction. Heresy, surely? Was nothing sacred? The rest, Frank Clark's Tribesmen, now a minority within the ground, did their best to raise the atmosphere and get some vocal support behind the team. But it made little difference. The silence was at times deafening. The roar that would once have taken the roof off the Gallowgate End, had one existed, was now little more than a faint cry. The gentrification of St. James' Park was complete!

Meanwhile, the draw for the third round of the FA Cup had given the pessimists even more reason to feel suicidal. Blackburn at home - the tie of the round. But on current form they would murder us, they had nearly beaten us at St. James' Park in the league back in October when we were on top form. The outcome this time didn't bear thinking about, and the fact that we could have gone from major contenders in four competitions to completely bust in just nine weeks was a scenario no one was even prepared to discuss! Practically the whole Toon Army believed that our number was up, that we would get knocked out and be left a week into the new year with only a place in next season's UEFA Cup to play for.

At least the *coup de gras* was delayed for a further nine days. Against the odds, although quite fairly on the balance of play, we managed a draw and lived to fight another day. A second half strike by Lee, cutting inside his marker at the Gallowgate End, secured the replay but there was still little room for optimism. If we couldn't beat Blackburn at home what chance did we have at Ewood Park? Not since that last minute Liam O'Brien strike had undone Rovers in September 1990 had we gained anything there. The three games since had all ended in defeat and their prolific strikeforce, Shearer and Sutton, the SAS, were taking no prisoners on their home turf.

Standing in the Corner

The wait for the replay felt merely like a stay of execution. On a cold January night, the Sky Sports cameras were poised to record in all its grisly detail the final destruction of the spent force that was Newcastle United. The fact that Sky had now given up on us, the same organisation that had hailed us as 'The Entertainers' not twelve months before, was a stark forewarning as to our probable fate. But, turning the formbook on its head, United refused to roll over as the whole world seemed to expect. We gave as good as we got in the opening sixty minutes, taking the game to the champions-elect in a pulsating and classic cup tie. Nevertheless, for that first hour there was still the nagging feeling that we would catch a sucker punch. Just then there was a brief glimmer of the sort of radiant form that had lit up the first three months of the season. Reacting quickly to a clearance from a corner, Marc Hottiger caught the dropping ball full volley and powered a thirty-yard thunderbolt straight into the bottom corner of the Blackburn net. Game on! Rovers responded like men possessed, pouring forward in waves, conscious that their double aspirations were now in real danger. The Magpies defended tigerishly, but ten minutes from time the inevitable equaliser came. Now the match seemed sure to go into extra-time.

Enter Newcastle's most unlikely hero. Lee Clark had begun his professional career billed as the next Paul Gascoigne and had become a genuine star during the promotion season of two years before. Now his chances had become limited with the increasing depth of the squad and he would never have a better opportunity to show his worth to a side top-heavy in the attacking midfield department. Nicknamed "Jigsaw" because of his tendency to 'go to pieces in the box', Clarkie was about to show uncharacteristic composure in front of goal. Reacting quickest to a ball into the area that the ordinarily adept Blackburn defence should have dealt with, Clarkie took a couple of strides forward and stroked the ball confidently into the net. 2-1! Against all expectations we were through to Round Four and a home tie with Swansea City. That dream of a trophy season was back on!

But if Newcastle's form was showing signs of an upturn, that of our star striker was still very much in the doldrums. Andy Cole hadn't found the net since November 26th, although part of the reason was his repeated absence from first team action because of shin splints. Paul Kitson had come into the side, and whilst his presence seemed to lack the menace of Coley at his best, his current form was at least as good. Kevin Keegan had made no secret of his admiration for QPR's robust forward Les Ferdinand, and it was known that Rangers were resigned to losing their man in the summer. The winds of change were blowing, but no one seriously believed that it would be Cole that would make way for Sir Les. Especially not midway through the season, with us still in the FA Cup and matters to be resolved in the league. Then the bombshell was dropped! Halfway through the week before the crunch return match at home to Manchester United, rumours started to fly around that Cole was on his way to Old Trafford. I was at work when the rumour broke, midway through a Tuesday afternoon. My new workplace, a penicillin factory on the south Northumberland coast, received the bulk of its deliveries immediately after lunch and a lorry driver, apparently a Mackem, had broken the news at the gatehouse.

"Utter bollocks!" I concluded when confronted with the rumour. Many Sunderland fans, now having to endure the misery of their rivals being on a different planet, had resorted to concocting outlandish stories in the hope of fooling the occasional Magpie! This tale was the tallest yet. But the longer the afternoon wore on, the more the saga continued. I was starting to believe there might be a grain of truth in the report, like an agreement between the two clubs that Cole would move in the summer. But in those days, with the Internet in its infancy, there wasn't the instant medium to find out the truth. I had to wait until three o'clock and the hourly news on Radio Five. F***ing Hell! It was unbelievable. The whole thing was true!

Of course, there was utter pandemonium once the news was confirmed. Rumour and counter-rumour about what had prompted the sale spread like wildfire across the site, all complete bunkum dreamt up by punters whose background was the bookies, not the football ground. Down the road in Newcastle, there was even greater uproar. Fans gathered on the steps at the back of the Milburn Stand demanding an explanation, in scenes reminiscent of the 'Sack the Board' days. To fans of old, the outward transfer of a star player brought back nightmares of those terrible times. What was going on? The days of Newcastle United, the selling club, were supposed to be over. In a bid to pacify the crowd, Keegan emerged from his office deep inside the ground and appeared on the steps to explain his reasoning. That, at least, was a change from the stoney-walled silence that had been the response to fans' anger in the past. But however sincere his response, KK was unable to convince the stunned supporters. He was, of course, powerless to confirm that the six million pound transfer money would eventually be converted into the more versatile Les Ferdinand. Or to predict that, over the next season and a half, the form of the £1 million makeweight in the deal, right-winger Keith Gillespie, would eclipse that of £7 million-rated Cole. The fans remained unswayed and bitterly disappointed at the sale of their star.

European Dreams

For the Manchester United game, both Cole and Gillespie were sidelined by contractual agreement, and the 1-1 draw did neither side any favours as Blackburn stole further ground in their singular quest for the title. The championship was now nothing more than memory for Newcastle, but at least that dreary form of Christmas was left behind as 1995 got going. In the Premiership, 16 points from a possible 21 were taken in the next seven games, not enough to threaten the leaders, but sufficient to keep us sitting pretty in third place. Two further home wins ensured that we reached the last eight in the FA Cup. Swansea City were overwhelmed 3-0 and then, at last, Alan Ball's sky blue charges defeated 3-1 with a spectacular fluke giving John Beresford his first ever United goal from open play. The reward was a sixth round draw away at Everton. Tough, but surely nothing like as hard as having to go and get a result at Blackburn!

The whole mood of the Toon Army had become more upbeat. The midwinter crisis was forgotten, the offloading of Andy Cole a little easier to accept as rumours of a summer transfer bonanza grew. For the time being, things were starting to smell of roses again, even if a 0-2 reverse at Liverpool on March 4th saw us slip behind Frank Clark's Nottingham Forest into fourth place. That didn't really matter. Anything down as far as fifth would be good enough for Europe, provided that the Reds were one of the teams in the top five. Roy Evans' Anfield men had already won the League Cup, guaranteeing their UEFA Cup slot. The only real danger was Leeds, languishing in sixth, the best part of ten points behind us. Eight days after the Liverpool disappointment, though, came a far heavier Merseyside hammer blow for Newcastle United. Without ever creating more than a half-chance, we were dumped out of the FA Cup by a headed goal from Everton's Duncan Ferguson. The last chance of silverware in 95-96 had gone and we were left with the consolation of attempting to salvage a UEFA Cup place from a season that had promised so much more. In the weeks that followed our FA Cup exit, however, we were about to make a pig's ear of even that seemingly easy task.

Nonetheless, progress immediately following our cup defeat had been promising, with home wins over West Ham and Arsenal. The FA Cup may have gone, but Europe was still very much on the cards. On Wednesday 22nd March, the opening day of the trout season, I had gone fishing as usual, and on returning to the car tuned the radio in for news of our midweek away game at Southampton. Within five minutes of starting the engine, I heard the news I was hoping for - we were winning 1-0 through a goal from Kitson with twenty minutes remaining. The Saints hadn't looked like scoring all night. It seemed we were on course, at least, to emulate our UEFA Cup qualification of the previous campaign. I continued onward on my thirty-minute journey, hoping there wouldn't be any further news from The Dell until I was five minutes from home. Some hope. Southampton scored three times in the last ten minutes in a typical Newcastle United exhibition on how to concede late goals! Two weeks later, we dropped another unlikely three points, losing again at Goodison Park, this time 0-2, with Robert Lee sent off. Leeds had now closed the gap to just two points, with a monumental six-pointer against them to come on Saturday April 17th.

It is almost always the case in a crunch match that a team in form holds the whip-hand over an opponent whose form is patchy. They have the initiative and confidence, whereas the struggling side often lacks self-belief. That was certainly the scenario at St. James' Park on that bright April day. Newcastle had been knocked out of the UEFA, League and FA Cups,

European Dreams

all by supposedly inferior opposition. We had blown a five-point advantage in the Premiership and been overtaken, not just by Blackburn and Man United, but also by Forest and even now by Liverpool. If we lost today, we would slip back into sixth and be passed by Leeds. The magnitude of such an occurrence was lost on nobody. Not only would we have forsaken all that silverware, we would have slipped out of the places for next season's UEFA Cup. Such an event was unthinkable. Leeds by contrast had nothing to lose. Their run of form had taken them from nowhere to the brink of European qualification, success they had been denied since their League Championship of three years before. Leeds were self-assured, Newcastle edgy and by the hour mark the Yorkshire side's superiority was underlined by a 0-1 scoreline. We had dominated possession but our attacks were getting us nowhere, breaking down like they had in the dark months of winter as the final ball went astray. Then we were thrown a lifeline. Twenty-one yea -old left-back Robbie Elliot, a survivor of the Ardiles days, scored an unlikely equaliser and the whole picture had changed. If things stayed as they were, we would retain our two-point advantage over our rivals with a much easier run-in. All we needed to do was shut up shop and hold out for the last ten minutes. Of course, that is never the Newcastle United way. Within minutes of scoring we were undone as a defensive lapse let in Leeds' mercurial striker Tony Yeboah. The African rounded Srnicek and slotted the ball home - 2-1 Leeds. It was a hard road back for the Magpies this time, as Leeds' grit and determination saw them survive the onslaught of the last five minutes. For the second time that season we had been knocked out of Europe by slackness at the back. The fine line between entertaining football and its kamikaze equivalent had never been so stark!

Standing in the Corner

The shock of the Leeds defeat was too much for a demoralised Newcastle. One by one we had been denied our aspirations with the final insult of losing the one thing we had taken for granted, qualification for Europe. The defeat had knocked the stuffing out of a United side that had been deprived of two key players by injury all season, and had played most of it with no prolific goalscorer. In some ways, it was little wonder that we had blown so many rewards and no surprise in the final four games of 1994-95 that we failed to overhaul Leeds' single point advantage. It seemed our bitter destiny that even the late salvation of a Manchester United FA Cup success was to be undone. With Blackburn having lifted the Premiership title, a win for the Red Devils over our conquerors Everton would have opened the back door for us into the UEFA Cup. But even that wasn't to be. A Paul Rideout goal lifted the Cup for the Toffees and we were left in limbo for another twelve months. The final match of 1995-96, a 3-2 win over relegated Crystal Palace, ended with the now traditional lap of honour round the completely enclosed St. James' Park. But it was a more subdued occasion than the one exactly a year before. We had come to expect 'success' of one form or another, but this season we hadn't achieved anything that finishing eighteenth wouldn't have equalled.

Of course it was disappointing. Keegan was to say, much later, that it would have been far more satisfying if the league placings of 94-95 and the season before could have been swapped around. Simple logic, but a man of Keegan's experience must have known that in reality the season just passed represented one step forward, not two back. The squad was stronger and there was still money in the kitty for further signings. Keegan's gamble in selling Andy Cole would soon pay off in the shape of Les Ferdinand as well as the added bonus that was Keith Gillespie. The problem was that the club was now a business hankering after the

European Dreams

affections of club-shop-dwelling free-market consumers. For them, sixth place was five worse than winners and, more critically, not even good enough for Europe. In most cases their verdict was "must do better" and if things didn't improve, they would just take their custom elsewhere. I for one wished that they would all p*** off!

For the terrace-reared aficionado of the old school, however, the season's achievements had to be taken in greater context than just by comparison with the one before. Sixth-top of the Premiership was a sight more convincing than bottom of the old First Division, or twentieth in the league below. Add in the UEFA Cup campaign and domestic cup runs of greater duration than anything since 1976 and it was plain to see that Newcastle United was moving forwards, not back. On the contrary, it was time to feel proud to be a Newcastle supporter. Think of how we had felt, by comparison, in 1978, 1989 and 1990.

As we filed out of the ground for the last time that season, the two words on the lips of everyone were 'What if?' What if Albert and Sellars hadn't got injured when they did? What if we hadn't conceded those two late goals at home to Bilbao? What if we hadn't sold Andy Cole and what if there had been a bit of atmosphere inside the stadium when things hadn't been going so well??? It was a rhetorical conundrum racking the brains of each and every Toon Army regular as they marched away from another season at St. James' Park. All except one, that is. The 'what ifs?' going through my mind bore relation to a far bigger picture. They were about the last twenty seasons or so of Newcastle United's history and the fact that this, in terms of league and cup, had been about the best out of any during that period. How had we reached the point we were at? How could we have got there earlier or might we have even never made it at all?

Standing in the Corner

What if Gordon Lee had never happened to Newcastle United? What if Arthur Cox had stayed? What if we had never sold Waddle, Beardsley and Gascoigne, or what if we had been relegated in 1992? It was all as much of a mystery as the issues vexing the rest of the Newcastle supporters now arriving back at their cars, at the bus stop or in the Metro station. In fact there were only two questions I could answer affirmatively. What was the greatest victory I had seen in that time? Taken in context, it had to be Liverpool away in October 1988. And the worst defeat? This answer was even more obvious, but the twist in its tail had the sweetest irony. Losing to Sunderland in the play-offs of 1990 forced the old guard to invite John Hall onto the board in the wake of two disastrous seasons. Had we won, we would have been promoted and the Magpie Group's bid for control dead in the water. The sequence of events that followed would almost certainly have paralleled those of 1984 to 89, only it probably wouldn't have taken five years for us to go back down.

Trying to cram the turning points of nearly a quarter of a century into a thought process lasting the time it took to walk to the Haymarket was giving me a headache. Why not sit down and write a book about it? That way, I could take a leisurely nine years. I needed somewhere to find inspiration, though, and the wooden-floored Irish theme bars that littered Newcastle city centre in the mid-Nineties were not the place.

At least there was still somewhere I could recall the good old days - times when I'd longed for Newcastle to have a top-six team and a stadium to be proud of. The Labour Club had hardly changed at all since the mid-Eighties, except that the bar was now decorated with pictures of Waddle, Beardsley, Gazza et al, circa 84-88. Why, there was even a glimpse of Jack Charlton on one old photo, whatever happened to him? As I chewed the fat over a pint with other fans that had been there, seen it and done it, there was one thing we were all agreed on. The next twenty years would have to be eventful to live up to the twenty that had just gone!